marilyn
MONROE

ROGER BAKER

Design
Design Box

Photographs
UPI/Bettmann, New York
Photofest, New York
Vintage Magazine Co, London

Picture Research
Leora Kahn
Jean Gale

Commissioning Editor
Andrew Preston

Publishing Assistant
Edward Doling

Editorial
Scott Coombs
Fleur Robertson

Production
Ruth Arthur
David Proffit

Director of Production
Gerald Hughes

Director of Publishing
David Gibbon

CLB 2396
© 1990 Colour Library Books Ltd, Godalming, Surrey, England.
All rights reserved.
This 1990 edition published by Crescent Books,
distributed by Crown Publishers, Inc,
225 Park Avenue South, New York, New York 10003.
Printed and bound in Italy.
ISBN 0 517 69326 7
h g f e d c b a

marilyn
MONROE

ROGER BAKER

PORTLAND HOUSE

CONTENTS

The time: summer, 1985. The place: a central London cinema that specialized in late-night showings of classic and cult movies. That night it was to be *Some Like It Hot*, considered by many to be Marilyn Monroe's greatest film.

A packed audience of young people – most of whom were probably not even born when Marilyn Monroe died in 1962 – sat attentively through the film's opening sequence, waiting for Marilyn's first entrance. She arrives, breathless and late for the train which will take her and the all-girl band to Florida. As she wiggles and totters along the platform, the train lets out a belch of steam which makes her jump and twist her hips in alarm, a movement which is at the same time hilarious and sexy.

At this point the audience broke into spontaneous applause.

No other screen star – living or dead – has achieved such a lasting impact, has been able to stimulate such an expression of warmth, affection and sheer delight as Marilyn Monroe. And she seems to grow in stature with every year that has passed since her death.

What makes her unique is more than the various essential qualities she undoubtedly possessed. It is, rather, their combination. That celebrated wriggle in *Some Like It Hot*, for example, is both funny and voluptuous – two qualities which, convention says, cannot go together since they cancel each other out. Monroe could also be, at the same time, innocent and experienced, vulnerable and threatening, waif and tigress, girl next door and femme fatale, child and woman. It has often been said that women warmed to her, that men did not just want to go to bed with her, but to protect her and look after as well. Individual members of her audiences, it seemed, took hold of the qualities which most appealed to them.

Then there was her appearance – the vibrant halo of blonde hair and the lusciously perfect body that looked as good in the nude sequences of her final, uncompleted film, *Something's Got to Give*, as in the notorious nude calendar shot she posed for back in 1949, thirteen years earlier.

Here we find another interesting paradox. Although nobody can deny that Monroe had natural assets in abundance, many women have started out with more and achieved less. Her screen image was painstakingly created over the years with the aid of a little plastic surgery to nose and jaw, a little dental work, a reassessment of her hairline and a continued coloring of her hair. And yet there never seemed to be anything the least bit artificial or contrived about the way she looked – even when made up to the hilt for a film or a personal appearance.

Just as a basic, endearing quality of innocence always shone through even her most complex performances, so the basic, healthy, sparkling beauty of the natural all-American girl shone through the artifice of surgeon, designer, hairdresser and make-up artist.

Of the twenty-nine films Marilyn Monroe made, perhaps only half a dozen stand up to critical examination – and even in the classic *Bus Stop* allowance has to be made for the film's period. Such a comparatively small output of truly memorable work seems disproportionate to the extent of her fame and the growth of her posthumous celebrity. Over the years she has become an eternal icon: a symbol, an image, a shrine.

This elevation from screen actress and pin-up to goddess may have been started by the now-famous silk screen prints that the late Andy Warhol made soon after her death. He, more than anyone, fixed her face as the pre-eminent symbol of America's move from the straight-laced 1950s into the liberated 1960s. In his book, *Marilyn in Art*, Roger G. Taylor collects more than a hundred paintings of Monroe, ranging from posters, fanzines stuff cartoons to more formal art gallery material, a collection which reveals more than anything the depths to which that face has penetrated the psyche of painters, graphic artists and designers – and consequently of the world at large.

And in this context it must be remembered that Monroe began her career as a photographer's model. It was work she obviously enjoyed, submitting herself gladly to the camera at every opportunity and drawing superb work from such distinguished photographers as Richard Avedon, Eve Arnold, Bert Stern and Cecil Beaton. Even the casual flash photographs snapped at press receptions

and airports invariably reveal her extraordinary beauty and presence. Artists have used her to portray virtually every facet, not only of her own character but of the character of the eternal woman. And most of the paintings were made after her death.

In 1989, an exhibition of the photography of Inge Morath, who married Arthur Miller after his final separation from Monroe, included a poignant shot of the star working on her last completed film, *The Misfits*. "Do we need yet another photograph of Marilyn Monroe?" asked one commentator tetchily; a question to which the public simply answered, "Yes!"

Monroe was infinitely greater than the sum of her parts, and her character has contributed as much to her legendary status as anything else. Since her death millions of words have been written trying to analyze and explain the mystery of her personality. In the early years of her career she was seen as a tiresome, empty-headed, sexually rapacious climber, good for a laugh but hardly to be taken seriously as either a woman or an actress. By the time *Some Like It Hot* was released in 1959, Monroe had achieved several pinnacles. She was acknowledged as Hollywood's reigning sex queen, probably the best-known film star in the world. She had proven indisputably that she must be taken seriously as an actress (though there were a few who remained unconvinced), married two of the most celebrated men in America, and starred opposite Laurence Olivier, the world's greatest actor. She also formed her own production company – the first Hollywood star to do so, and an early, significant signal of the way in which the industry would develop in the future.

And then, a mere three years later, at the time of her death, the picture looked slightly different. *Some Like It Hot* was followed by the indifferent *Let's Make Love* and the unexpected *The Misfits*, a script by her then-husband Arthur Miller and a film which puzzled many of her most loyal fans. She had been through a passionate but ultimately disastrous relationship with Yves Montand, her co-star in *Let's Make Love*, and had divorced Arthur Miller. She was becoming conscious of the passing years and was becoming increasingly jealous of Elizabeth Taylor, whom she saw as her only dangerous rival, and desperately needed a vehicle to restore her prestige and confidence. She was plagued by illnesses (major and minor) and was becoming more dependant on alcohol and tranquilizers. She was living alone in a gloomy little house tucked away in Brentwood, a suburb of Los Angeles.

Many commentators have read this as a scenario for suicide: the goddess slipping from her throne and seeing before her nothing but an abyss. But Monroe had seen tough times before (and without the authority she now possessed to help her survive). The house she bought was the very first home she had ever owned (her life had been spent in other people's houses, in hotels and hostels). Her sex life was taking an upward turn and she had been re-hired by Twentieth Century Fox to complete *Something's Got to Give* and was slimming and preparing herself for the role.

All these high and low points in Monroe's career were, of course, widely reported and would be known to the public. But, inevitably, the public's information was drawn from superficial and not always friendly sources – from newspaper articles, gossip columns, quick exchanges at airports, "exclusive" interviews and the often exaggerated, if not plainly false hand-outs supplied by the film studios. So, a fairly detailed but essentially superficial profile of Marilyn Monroe was created.

Just as one of her screen talents was the ability to persuade every onlooker that she was exactly what that person wanted her to be, so in life every member of the public decided that Monroe was what he or she wanted her to be. To some she was as promiscuous as a bunny rabbit, while others swore she was dedicated to finding a monogamous love relationship. To some she was just an empty-headed bimbo who could not keep two consecutive thoughts in her head, while others saw her as a serious student of acting and a tenacious seeker of cultural aspirations. Some saw her as the helpless victim of Hollywood and its ruthless star system, others as one who manipulated that system for her own ambitions.

Rumor, gossip and conjecture surrounded her

until her sudden, unexpected death jolted Hollywood and the world into a shuddering silence. During the course of one tragic night her status changed from leading film star to icon.

The mere fact that she was dead was shocking enough: a beautiful young woman who, through the cinemas, had given immeasurable delight to millions and who was at the peak years of her career was suddenly dead. The first news was confusing. She had been found on her bed in a locked room, naked, clutching a telephone. Had she taken a deliberate overdose, or an accidental one? The telephone suggested she was calling for help. Was it suicide, or a ghastly mistake?

The autopsy and inquest were no help, in fact they added to the mystery and confusion, and almost at once there were enough puzzles surrounding her death to create more than usual interest. There was confusion about the actual time of her death, about who was in the house and how she was found, about who she was trying to telephone. There were conflicting statements by those close to her and certain obvious investigations were not carried out. Today most of these mysteries remain unsolved and, despite the tenacious and thorough sleuthing conducted by investigative journalists, will probably stay that way.

Eventually the suspicion that the actress was murdered began to take hold. The darker corners of her life were explored, tenuous connections with the Mafia were discovered, and so were her relationships with the Kennedy brothers (President John F. Kennedy and Attorney-General Robert F. Kennedy), which sent conjecture along several political routes right up to the White House itself. If Monroe was murdered, then by whom and for what reason will probably never be conclusively settled. As we shall see, one or two investigators have proved it to their own satisfaction – but the problems of solving a mystery death almost three decades old (with most major witnesses now dead) are virtually insurmountable.

With her death, the Marilyn Monroe industry began and within a year the biographies started to appear; some cheap and flashy, some thoughtful and considered. And they keep on coming, those biographies, and all the biographers offer their own interpretation of the elusive star. Sometimes they vary considerably but one way or another the detailed, intimate life of this star of stars began to be revealed.

It is not the purpose of this short review of Marilyn Monroe's life and work to open up new controversies, or to take any specific standpoint about her as woman or actress. What it will do is present a straightforward account of her life and career with accuracy, summarize those controversial moments of her life where interpretations differ, and offer fans, old and new, a portrait of the kind of star the like of whom we shall not see again.

CHAPTER

I

Norma Jeane Baker, the girl who was later to become Marilyn Monroe, was born on 1 June 1926. "I'm a Gemini. That means intellect," she once breathed to an interviewer. But it is also the sign of the Twins, and many biographers have discovered that one important clue to the way in which Marilyn conducted her life, and reacted to events around her, is that she was always conscious of being two people. This does not mean that she was schizophrenic in any technical way, nor that she displayed contrasting personalities as the popular view of that term suggests. It means, more simply, that she never forgot her childhood and the person she was before the transformation into Marilyn Monroe took place.

A typical example is found in the story that early in her film career she was, naturally enough, excited to spot her name in big letters on the marquee of the cinema showing her movie. She stared at it, drove round the block and had another look. Later she commented: "I just wished it had said 'Norma Jeane' so that the kids I was at school with would know it was me!" Towards the end of her life, another reporter asked her what Geminis were like. "Jekyll and Hyde. Two in one," she replied. "I wish I were just me!" The "me" was always Norma Jeane; Marilyn Monroe was the glittering shell which surrounded that eternal child, the carefully and cleverly constructed artefact that the public fell in love with.

It is, incidentally, only in the last few years that the final "e" has been restored to her name "Jeane." One of her best biographers, Fred Lawrence Guiles called his book *Norma Jean* simply because, like many of Marilyn's friends, and at least two of her husbands, he assumed that is how it was spelled. Later he discovered that Marilyn herself consistently used the unconventional spelling and he restored that for the revised edition of his book in 1985. "It is my hope that this present work will give currency to Marilyn's preference," he writes in that edition. It did, and all Marilyn commentators since have spelt her name as she would have wished.

During her lifetime – and for many years after her death – much was made by writers and commentators of Marilyn Monroe's unhappy and deprived childhood. Certainly she grew up under circumstances which few parents would want for their daughters, but her life was not quite as Dickensian as some (including Monroe herself) would have us believe. The first official studio biography that was issued about her in 1946 had her father die in a car crash soon after she was born and her mother too ill to look after her. She was, therefore, adopted by family friends. Five years later, in 1951, a further biography repeats this information adding that Marilyn never knew either of her parents. Although not explicitly stated, the reader is left with the impression of a hapless orphan cast on the goodwill of Los Angeles County.

In interviews the young starlet tended to add touches of color to this basic plot. She claimed her grandmother tried to smother her with a pillow when she was barely a year old, she spoke of being forced to wash dishes in an orphanage, she included memories of being abused by the father in one of the families in whose care she was placed, of being raped by a policeman.

The star and her studios, it seems, were in collusion to reconstruct her actual childhood experience – never straying too far from the truth, but adding emphases here and there to make the saga more pathetic, more touching and the spectacle of her rising stardom, therefore, more impressive. Going from cast-out orphan to goddess was a progress which would excite that most basic of American aspirations. If any man could become president, then any woman could become Marilyn Monroe.

The Los Angeles into which Norma Jeane was born was, of course, very different from the massive, heartless sprawl we know today. In the

A routine studio publicity shot, perhaps, but a photograph that conjures all the charm, sexuality and sheer allure that was Marilyn Monroe at the height of her success.

1920s, the area was dominated by the big film studios churning out countless films. The big stars demonstrated their position and wealth with their spectacular houses placed among the canyons and hills. Elsewhere it was a patchwork of small frame houses, set back to back but with squares of garden backing up to each other. Though they were cramped to a certain extent and had only basic facilities, these townships were not slums, nor were they threaded with violence and extreme poverty. There was warmth, neighborliness and a pleasant atmosphere.

But Los Angeles was also a melting pot, a focus for the unsettled, for migrants from Europe, the north, Mexico and the East Coast. The 1920s was a liberating time as women began to find autonomy for the first time, and men began to take off, disappear and move around with no commitment. Divorce was common, single women earning a living and looking after their own children was far from unusual.

Such a person was Norma Jeane's mother, Gladys Baker. She was born in Mexico in 1900 and married Jack Baker when she was still a teenager, soon producing two children, Hermitt and Bernice. By the time she was twenty-six and Norma Jeane was born, Baker and the two children had disappeared from her life. She had married again, this time to Edward Mortenson, but he had also abandoned her. Gladys had a good job, working as a film cutter with Consolidated Film Industries in Hollywood.

Despite the liaison with Mortenson, Gladys commonly called herself Baker. She was in her mid-twenties, bright, competent and certainly attractive. She is said to have looked like Hollywood's reigning beauties Gloria Swanson and Norma Talmadge, and it is clear from photographs that the young Gladys had looks and style. One can assume that, at this time, she was in charge of herself and embarked on an affair with a man she was working alongside, C. Stanley Gifford.

It will probably never be known which man was actually Norma Jeane's father. Some sources have Mortenson taking off long before the child could have been conceived, and the consensus seems to be that Gifford was the man. It is said

that when Gladys's colleagues made a collection for her, Gifford refused to contribute and, in fact, disappeared before the child was born. In his important 1960 biography, *Marilyn Monroe*, Maurice Zolotov includes this remark from one of Gladys's co-workers: "She was a beautiful woman, one of the most beautiful women it was ever my privilege to know. She had a good heart and was a good friend and always happy ...."

But now this happy, beautiful woman had a problem in the form of a lively, chunky, bouncing baby girl. Finding it difficult to continue working and at the same time bring up a baby single-handedly, she found a foster home for Norma Jeane and paid the family $25 a week to look after the child.

That Norma Jeane never knew who her real father was is true. But the story that her mother was an invalid, too ill to look after her and therefore abandoned her is a long way from what really happened. It is clear that Gladys never wanted to part from her baby. She visited her at the foster home regularly and when Norma Jeane was ill took three weeks off work to look after her personally.

Gladys had a project she was working on, which was quite simply to provide herself with a husband, a home, a father for her child. This should not have been too difficult considering Gladys's personal attractiveness, her independent status and earning capacity. Although she had a series of male friends over the next few years she never re-married, but her aim to live in her own house with her daughter was realized. After eight years Gladys had saved enough money to put a down-payment on a bungalow in Hollywood. She rented out the house, but rented back a couple of rooms for her and Norma Jeane. The longed-for family life (although there was no husband and father) began to happen.

But, unfortunately, this happy state of affairs did not last long. In 1935 Gladys had a nervous breakdown, was taken to Los Angeles General Hospital and later placed in Norwalk State Asylum where she was diagnosed as a paranoid schizophrenic.

The family to whom Gladys had rented her bungalow worked in the film industry. They were an English couple with a grown daughter.

He was the stand-in for the celebrated star George Arliss, and she was what was known as a "dress extra"; that is, she had walk-on parts in drawing-room comedies which needed a touch of class and style in the background. Their daughter eventually became the stand-in for the beautiful Madeleine Carroll.

When Gladys was whisked off to hospital, this family displayed great affection towards Norma Jeane. They retained the house and looked after the child. They sold some of the furniture to keep up the mortgage payments and may have applied to the county for additional support for the child. (Norma Jeane became an official "county child" a couple of years later.) But this arrangement did not last long either. Arliss retired and the stand-in lost his job. The family moved into furnished accommodation taking Norma Jeane with them, but eventually decided that they would have to return to England and Norma Jeane was once again left to the mercy of the state and neighbors.

The family which fostered the baby Norma Jeane for $25 a week, and with whom she lived for the first seven and a half years of her life, were Ida and Albert Wayne Bolender. Some Monroe biographers have painted the Bolenders black, but there seems to be no objective evidence for this. The worst that has been said about them is that they were religious fundamentalists and this means, of course, that theirs was not exactly a fun house. In her later years Marilyn was to say that all she remembered about them was salvation and the strap.

But as we know, the grown-up Marilyn was prone to fantasy and the ordinary, commonplace cuffs and spankings handed out to naughty children were common to all families, religious or not. In fact it seems that the Bolenders looked after the little Norma Jeane to the best of their ability and according to their own lights. At the same time, the Bolenders were fostering a small boy, called Lester and he and Norma Jeane were, inevitably, companions and playmates at this time.

So maybe the household had strict rules about such things as popular music, alcohol, good behavior and obedience. But against this background Norma Jeane seems to have enjoyed a happy enough childhood. Certainly photographs show a perky, well-dressed child. There were toys and parties, trips to the sea-side and a pet dog. This hound – called Tippy – met the end most town dogs meet and was run over one night when out on its prowls. Some stories say a neighbor attacked it with a spade. In later years, Ida Bolender would say that she and her husband wanted formally to adopt the young Norma Jeane, but Gladys would not allow this – she was, after all, working towards getting herself and her child under one family roof.

There was, however, one unhappy incident which blemished these years. This concerned Norma Jeane's maternal grandmother, Della Hogan Monroe. She had been born in Missouri in 1876. Like so many other families, the Hogans were driven by poverty to move west and seek work in California. In 1899 Della married Otis Elmer Monroe and they moved to Mexico where Gladys was born.

Both Della and Otis were in a precarious mental state and eventually drifted apart. By the time her granddaughter was born Della had returned from a trip to India where she had followed her third husband (a man called Grainger, an oil engineer) and had established herself in Hawthorne, across the way from the Bolender house. She had also joined the evangelist Four Square Gospel Church, founded by Aimee Semple McPherson.

Her marital problems, plus the exposure of McPherson as a religious fraud seem to have tipped Della's precarious mental state into insanity at this time. Having her grandmother across the road was no help to the young Norma Jeane. The older woman – only 51 but with the fierce, distracted look of the unstable – varied in her attitudes, at one moment smothering Norma Jeane with affection, the next throwing hysterical fits on the sidewalk. She was finally committed to Norwalk State Hospital where she died of a heart attack during a severe mental breakdown only a few days later.

So naturally when, a few years later, her own mother was committed to the same hospital it would be brought home to the young girl that insanity, of one form or another, was present in her family.

Lester Bolender was another foster child (legally adopted), the same age as Norma Jeane and her first playmate. They were often mistaken for twins.

When Norma Jeane's mother was working as a film cutter at Columbia Studios, she became close friends with a film librarian called Grace McKee whose help was invaluable during the time she was trying to find a home of her own. Eventually, Grace was made Norma Jeane's guardian until her twenty-first birthday.

After her mother was hospitalized, Norma Jeane continued to live with the English couple, and when they decided to return to England, Grace persuaded some neighbors to take Norma Jeane in. They were Mr. and Mrs. Harvey Giffen. He was a sound engineer in films and they had three children of their own.

This could have been the ideal situation for the child – a happy, close-knit family, comfortably off and loving. But Harvey Giffen was planning to leave Hollywood and find work in New Orleans, his hometown. He and his wife decided to adopt Norma Jeane and take her with them. At the same time, another couple, Mr. and Mrs. Reginald Carroll, were also happy to adopt Norma Jeane if her mother did not wish her to leave California.

As before, when the Bolenders had tried to adopt the child, Gladys out her foot down. Norma Jeane was definitely not up for adoption. Apparently, Gladys saw the requests as a threat to the one relationship in her life which was still capable of being retrieved. Maybe, in her lucid moments, she still envisaged herself and Norma Jeane together again in that home of their own. So Norma Jeane had nowhere to go and on 13 September 1935 she entered the Los Angeles Orphans Home Society where she lived for two years.

The shock of this sudden transition upon the child can only be imagined. Although she had never known the security and emotional stability of family life, Norma Jeane had been with a series of loving families enjoying the same freedoms that other children enjoyed, free to play, run around, dress up, have little adventures.

The orphanage was probably never as horrendous and cruel as the adult Marilyn (and many of her biographers) would have us believe. But it was regimented, monotonous, routine and drab. The food would be predictable and boring,

the staff would never have enough affection to spread among their charges. Certainly the experience was traumatic for Norma Jeane. The pitying looks of people as she and her companions walked to school hurt, as did the inescapable fact that she was not an orphan, a fact she knew well. Grace visited regularly, took her out – sometimes to the movies – and promised the child that one day soon she would be taken away from the orphanage.

By refusing to allow her daughter to be adopted, or to leave California, Gladys Baker effectively condemned the child to an uncertain and unsettled childhood. With one or two exceptions the various foster homes in which the growing Norma Jeane lived seem to have been kindly and nurturing. The Orphans' Home Society was on El Centro Avenue in the very heart of Hollywood and very close to the RKO studios. In later years Marilyn recalled how, after lights-out when the other children were asleep, she would hoist herself onto the dormitory window-ledge and gaze across at the brightly illuminated water tower of RKO and recall that her mother once worked there and that one day she herself would like to be a film star there.

The literal truth of this anecdote may be dubious – constructed as part of the Monroe legend which has the child ruthlessly determined to be a star from the age of nine. But it is far from unlikely that in the grey, restricted world in which she was living the bright lights of Hollywood represented the ultimate achievement. At Christmas the studio would invite the children from the orphanage over for the day, giving them little presents and ending the day with a screening of some appropriate movie. The connection with the film industry does run consistently through Norma Jeane's early life, so while she was in the orphanage it is not surprising that her one desire was to get out of the place and return to the freedoms of the non-institutionalized world outside.

During this time something of the future Marilyn became to emerge in the ten-year-old. She was growing up and had suddenly become taller than her contemporaries. She began to take an interest in her appearance, especially when on her visits Grace let her experiment with

Norma Jeane always had a natural affinity with the camera, which was quick to pick up on her knowing innocence and all-American freshness. It is interesting to compare this casual shot with the polished studio photographs that were to follow.

make-up. And she was also developing into an excellent athlete, preferring baseball and swimming. Several years later, when she was a model and then a starlet she would regularly run around the studio blocks every morning. All this early training probably had much to do with the eventual perfection of her body, not least in its ability to withstand the onslaughts of drugs and the many operations it was subjected to during Marilyn's adult years.

Eventually Grace did something about the situation. She conferred with the orphanage authorities and they all agreed that Norma Jeane would benefit from living with a family again. But Grace had her own problems. At the time she was trying to decide whether to marry a man who was courting her. He was Erwin Goddard (known as "Doc"), a divorced man with custody of his own three small children. Norma Jeane had met the Goddards and had established immediate rapport with them, especially the eight-year-old Beebe.

So Grace found herself in the position of having committed herself to taking on Norma Jeane before she had made a decision about her marriage. But she went ahead and in June 1937 Norma Jeane left the hated institution—not, however, for the security of Grace's home but once again for fostering by strangers. There followed what can only have been a most distressing six months for the child. The families with which she lived were quite unsatisfactory. One couple ran their own business which meant the child spent the summer holidays trapped in their car traveling all over Los Angeles County. Another simply took in county children for the sake of the subsistence grants that came with them and the husband was an alcoholic. Meanwhile Grace had married Doc Goddard and in January of 1938 brought Norma Jeane to live with them, an act which ushered in the most stable and rewarding period of her life.

The atmosphere in the household was pleasant and relaxed. Both Grace and Doc went out to work and although they were not well off they were comfortable enough to afford a few of life's minor pleasures. Norma Jeane entered Emerson Junior High School and at home had the companionship of Doc's daughter Beebe (eventually the two girls shared a bedroom). It was a close, friendly neighborhood and they got on with their nearest neighbors, a couple called Dougherty who had survived with dignity the very worst years of the Depression.

At this point another significant woman entered Norma Jeane's life. This was Grace's aunt, Ana Lower, a woman in her late fifties of whom Marilyn Monroe was later to say: "She was the first person in the world I ever really loved and she loved me. She was a wonderful human being ...." The relationship between the older woman and the developing child was close and very stable – and it stayed that way until Ana died in 1948 (before Marilyn had made any impact as a film star). The young Norma Jeane certainly saw the older woman as the first person she felt she could relate to as a mother-figure and "Aunt" Ana was continually supportive and helpful to the girl.

After an alleged incident in the Goddard household when Doc, slightly the worse for drink, made a clumsy pass at Norma Jeane she went to live with Aunt Ana for a while in her large new house in the wealthy Westwood suburb of Los Angeles. Ana introduced Norma Jeane to the Christian Science Church (founded by Mary Baker Eddy), which seemed, at that time, an ideal complement to the life she was leading. In fact, Norma Jeane remained a faithful church-goer for at least eight years.

During this period of course, the child was growing up, turning from schoolgirl into young woman. She transfered to Van Nuys High School and, when she was visiting or staying with Ana Lower, was mixing with a different type of person – the sons and daughters of people slightly higher up the social scale than the film industry workers she had previously known. She also began to take pride in her personal appearance.

The fully emerged Marilyn Monroe was regarded as a superb beauty. Claims have been made that in her early teens Norma Jeane was not particularly striking – not exactly plain, but ordinary looking with a stubby nose, weak chin and round face. Although she, and the studios, did make a few significant alterations to her face, early photographs tell a different story. Her hair

was a dull brown and tended to be straight, but it was regularly curled by Ana or Grace. Her face was roundish, but was transformed by her stunning smile. She grew to her full height – five feet, five inches – and her fondness for athletics paid its rewards with good proportion, good health and sensible eating habits.

Many biographers point out that during this period Norma Jeane's love of the movies seemed to take on an added edge. She went to the cinema regularly every Saturday and among her favorite stars were Norma Shearer, Bette Davis and Tyrone Power. On her bedroom wall hung a portrait of the greatest of her idols – Clark Gable. In fact she so infatuated with this actor that she would tell her schoolfriends that he was really her father. Twenty-three years later she would star with him in The Misfits – the last film either of them would make.

After the upheavals, uncertainties and insecurities of her early life it seemed at last that Norma Jeane had achieved a stable, tranquil existence. But already, what would be another major, crucial change was waiting in the wings.

A studio portrait taken when the newly named Marilyn Monroe had been taken on as a Twentieth Century Fox player. The hair has been blonded, the hairline itself adjusted, the eyebrows, nose and teeth slightly re-modeled. Everything from the neck down, however, was all her own work.

On 19 June, 1942 – barely two weeks after her sixteenth birthday – Norma Jeane Baker married twenty-one-year-old James E. Dougherty. The marriage was to last for four years and by the time the divorce was granted, in September 1946, Norma Jeane had become Marilyn Monroe.

As with most of the major events in Monroe's life, there are conflicting accounts of her first marriage. There is Dougherty's own version (which he published in *The Secret Happiness of Marilyn Monroe* in 1976), and the recollections that Marilyn herself would feed over the years to friends, journalists and anyone who would listen. It has sometimes been observed that Marilyn lied about her past (her "memories" of her time in the orphanage are typical). She did not lie to deceive, but rather to embroider, to exaggerate, to draw attention to herself and perhaps excite the love and pity of her friends and – through official studio biographies – her public. In Dougherty's case he would not, more than thirty years later, wish to present himself in anything but a favorable light.

Jim Dougherty was, literally, the boy next door. The garden of the house where he lived with his family backed up to the garden of the house where Norma Jeane was living with the Goddards. Grace Goddard and Mrs. Dougherty were chatting neighbors and, in downtown terms, Jim was one of the most eligible young men around. He had graduated from Van Nuys High School (where Jane Russell was a classmate). He was tall, athletic, had film-star good looks, went to church and worked at a Lockheed Aircraft plant alongside Robert Mitchum, who was later to become a powerful film actor and cast opposite Marilyn in *River of No Return*.

The chain of events which led to the marriage was set in motion when Doc Goddard applied for, and received, a job promotion which would relocate him in West Virginia. Grace announced they would be leaving and this meant that her guardianship of Norma Jeane would have to be legally terminated, once again leaving her to the mercy of the fates. One option could have been for Aunt Ana to take the teenager on, but this, apparently, was not considered (maybe Mrs. Lower considered herself too old). The other, far more likely option, was that Norma Jeane – who was fifteen at this time – would have to return to the orphanage which neither she nor her adoptive family liked to contemplate. So the time-honoured solution was sought – find her a husband.

This much seems factual enough. What is in dispute is the relationship between Norma Jeane and Jim Dougherty.

Marilyn's own view, which is one adopted, and embroidered on by her supporters, is that it was a calculated and arranged marriage, that she was railroaded into it (persuaded by fear of having to return into state care) and that Jim himself was pressured by Grace Goddard and his mother to aquiesce. Further, Marilyn was supposed to have never forgiven Grace for forcing her into this loveless marriage. She resented having to drop out of school to keep house and she was not at all interested in sex. Could she be married but stay "just friends" with her husband, she is reported to have asked Grace. Later she was to refer to her and Jim as "roommates with sex privileges."

Dougherty on the other hand asserts that once the possibility of marrying the girl next

One photographer who spotted the possibilities of the young Norma Jeane was Andre de Diennes, who placed her natural, youthful charm against the landscapes of California.

door came up and they started serious dating, that Norma Jeane was physically enthusiastic and quite assertive in securing and attracting his attention, and that their sex life was exciting and good. There is an often-repeated story that one day at work Dougherty produced a photograph of his young wife to show his workmate Robert Mitchum. In it Norma Jeane was wearing nothing but a smile.

It is only because of Norma Jeane's later fame as Marilyn Monroe that such a big deal is made of this marriage. Those were uncertain days, America was in the Second World War and austerity was beginning to bite. Thousands of young couples with minimal experience of life or love were pinning their fragile hopes for the future on each other. Many were to divorce later, but at the time Norma Jeane and Jim stood as good a chance as any of staying the course.

The wedding photographs show a charming and typical family group. Norma Jeane looks exquisite in a white lace gown, her dark blonde hair framing the heart-shaped face with a mass of curls. The handsome Jim looks at once protective and naive. Absent from the guest list were Grace and Doc Goddard (then in West Virginia) and Norma Jeane's mother Gladys who, after another relapse, had been committed to a sanatorium in San Francisco.

Monroe biographers who wish to disparage Jim Dougherty and present Norma Jeane as the victim of an arranged and loveless union tend to skip lightly over the first couple of years of their marriage. One who does not is Fred Lawrence Guiles whose biography, *Norma Jeane: The Life and Death of Marilyn Monroe*, is detailed and carefully researched. His portrait of the first two years of the marriage has charm and the ring of authenticity. There were problems and differences to come, major ones, but at first the young couple were quite happily making the best of their lot. One thing is certain – they were sexually entranced with each other. At home, in the car, even in backstreets they would make love, regardless of risk.

Their first home was a studio apartment and Norma Jeane's housekeeping was not exactly first-class. But then, she was only sixteen and had hardly any training for domesticity, no role-model mother to teach her about cleaning and cooking. But they managed in a happy-go-lucky sort of style and even managed to grab the occasional weekend away. On one of these Norma Jeane learned to ski – and found she had a natural ability for the sport. In fact, during the years of this marriage she spent quite a lot of time on sports, improving her swimming and taking up weight-lifting. Her athletic ability has been noted earlier. It was as if she was priming her body for the successes – and trials – to come.

It was, in many ways, a simple, rather ordinary life. But underneath a sense of strain was growing. One biographer writes: "It appears that Dougherty was a typical old-fashioned male chauvinist ..." which may be true but which has little meaning when considering the attitudes of a very young man in 1942. Jim in fact seems to have been a nice young man, but one with very definite ideas about how a wife should behave. Consequently Norma Jeane was not allowed to work, but had to stay at home, keep the place clean and be a housewife.

How far developed Norma Jeane's ideas of breaking into the film industry were at this time must remain unknown, but when at the beach or on weekends away, she was becoming aware of how attractive she was to men. During these years Norma Jeane grew up fast.

As the austerities of the war began to bite, life was not particularly easy and Jim, the all-American boy, began to feel he ought to be on active service. Much to his young wife's initial distress he joined the Merchant Marines. Norma Jeane was re-settled in his parents' house and he went off for training. After five weeks he was made a physical-training instructor, which meant he was attached to the base on Catalina Island, twenty-six miles off the Southern California coast, and that Norma Jeane could join him.

Another happy period began. Life for Norma Jeane at the base was attractive, the men admired her looks, there were parties, sporting activities and lots of sex for her and Jim – and again interpretations differ. One view is that Norma Jeane was getting frustrated and feeling restricted by the ordinariness of married life and and was getting edgy to feel a touch of freedom.

Her now-obvious sex appeal was upsetting Jim and he began to feel he could not hold her. The marriage was at the point of breakdown, so Jim himself applied for a transfer and was posted to Australia. The other view is that Norma Jeane was perfectly happy, deeply involved physically with Jim and starting to feel that her marriage would work. When Jim revealed that he was being shipped out she was devastated.

Whatever the truth, Jim did apply for the transfer himself and Norma Jeane returned to the Dougherty house to take up the role of war bride and dutiful daughter-in-law, keeping house while Ethel Dougherty maintained a full-time job as a nurse at the Radio Plane Company. This company, in Van Nuys, was run by the British actor Reginald Denny and made miniature planes used for target practice. It was not long before Norma Jeane, rapidly bored with her stultifying domestic role, asked her mother-in-law if she could find a place for her there. She could and Norma Jeane had her first job. At first she inspected the parachutes that were used to bring the target planes down gently. Later she was moved to the "dope" room where a liquid plastic was painted onto the outer covering of the little planes.

Although Jim had clearly released Norma Jeane's sexual nature, it seems she remained entirely faithful to him during his year-long absence. When not working she spent much time with Ana Lower and sometimes at the Dougherty house with her relations. When Jim finally returned for his first leave the young couple simply packed a couple of bags, left his parents' home and spent the weekend in a luxurious motel for, as one writer puts it, "a marathon sexual reunion." Norma Jeane took leave from Radio Plane for the three weeks of Jim's leave and they spent all the time together.

With hindsight it is possible to see that the marriage really ended when Jim first shipped out to Australia – the period of his leave was a passionate interlude. After he had returned, Norma Jeane resumed work at Radio Plane. But she also left the Dougherty house and moved in with Aunt Ana. She was about to embark on her first taste of freedom, to accept dates and enjoy herself; and within weeks the door which would lead to her future career was opened.

Throughout the Second World War, across all the nations involved, a pretty girl was regarded as the great morale booster for the troops. Apart from their initial erotic appeal, the young women whose pictures were tacked above bunks and pasted on the sides of planes represented everything the men were fighting for – the wife, mother, sister, girlfriend back home. As a result the pin-up picture was in great demand and as an industry the production of such work peaked. New faces were wanted everyday.

In July 1945, Ronald Reagan, who was a commanding officer at the First Motion Picture Unit, sent a photographer called David Conover to Radio Plane to take some publicity shots of women doing war work. Despite the dreariness of the setting, Conover instantly spotted the potential of Norma Jeane; and when she confided in him that she wanted to be a movie star he told her she would have to become a model first and that she certainly possessed all the right qualities to make a success of that.

He made a private assignment with her and they spent a few days in the Mojave Desert where he built up a portfolio of photographs of her posing against some of America's most thrilling landscapes. Unfortunately none of these shots survive – Conover later claimed the film was lost in the mail.

Norma Jeane then took sick leave from Radio Plane and approached the important Blue Book Modeling and Studio Agency where she was immediately accepted and put to work by the boss Emmeline Snively. In fact, Norma Jeane was able to pay the Agency for her tuition fees from her first modeling job.

Snively must take quite a lot of responsibility for the slow transformation of Norma Jeane into Marilyn Monroe. Perhaps her most notable move was to insist that Norma Jeane's dark (or "dirty") blonde hair be restyled and dyed to a full "blonde" blonde. She taught her how to smile without showing too many teeth, she laid the foundations for the famous Monroe walk and made suggestions about minor surgery to her face. Norma Jeane left her job at Radio Plane and became a full-time model and hostess at industrial shows, always popular, always in demand. Her image began to appear on the covers and inside innumerable magazines.

Pin-up, or cheesecake, photography in the mid-1940s was, by today's standards, quite innocent. Overt sexuality was played down and the emphasis was on wholesome, healthy girls who could be said to represent the innocence and vitality of America itself. Any erotic come-on was restricted to a certain glance of the eyes, a tantalizing smile full of promise. Norma Jeane at this time possessed all these qualities and the photographs of her at this time suggest a young woman that any lad would automatically treat with good manners and be quite happy to take home to mother.

There have been many attempts to analyze the qualities that made Marilyn Monroe into such a huge star, but inevitably they always return to her unique relationship with the camera. Not only did the camera like her – she liked it! Conover recalls that during his very first session with her at Radio Plane she was immediately involved, enthusiastic, making suggestions. Later he admired her stamina and dedication when they went on that extended shoot in the burning heat of the Mojave Desert and Death Valley. Throughout her career she was always ready to undertake lengthy and painstaking still sessions, and the portfolios of great photographers Cecil Beaton, Richard Avedon and Burt Stern among others include sensational studies of her. Even during the fraught and unhappy filming of *The Prince and the Showgirl* in London, she collaborated with the distinguished British cinematographer Jack Cardiff in a session which resulted in some of the most beautiful of all pictures of her. For someone who wants to be a film star, the ability to relate successfully with the camera is the prime requisite. From her very first months of modeling Norma Jeane proved that she had precisely that.

From this moment, the nineteen-year-old Norma Jeane was going to take charge of her own life. She left Radio Plane and she left her mother-in-law's house to move in with the encouraging and always supportive Aunt Ana – thus cutting off all links with the Dougherty family. The world of modeling captivated her and she soon became known as one of the

busiest on the West Coast. Meanwhile, at the other side of the world, Jim Dougherty seems to have no idea that he had lost his wife forever.

There has been considerable speculation about how Norma Jeane conducted her sex life during this period. Jim remained convinced that she could have been nothing else but faithful to him. But some things suggest otherwise. Typical is the arrival on the scene of a young Hungarian photographer called Andre de Dienes who took Norma Jeane out on long sessions in the desert and mountains. The photography reveals a gloriously happy girl-child in jeans and tied shirts, becoming a kind of natural extension of the majestic landscapes. Undoubtedly she and de Dienes became lovers on these trips. It is not cynical to suggest that there were other men.

That she would eventually become a major film star was the most predominant thought Norma Jeane's mind. She had confided in Emmeline Snively that she had a husband but this was kept dark. Talking with other ambitious models, Norma Jeane discovered that no studio would sign-up a young married woman who might have a baby. Something would have to be done about that.

Early in 1946 Norma Jeane's mother re-entered her life. She wanted to leave the San Francisco sanatorium and it was arranged that she would live with Norma Jeane in the flat at Aunt Ana's house. A tentative intimacy began between mother and daughter. Gladys's bid for freedom only lasted seven months but she was able to take care of the flat and answer the phone. There is also a touching story that she visited Emmeline Snively just to thank her for all she was doing for Norma Jeane.

Jim Dougherty returned on leave again and although it seems the couple resumed their uninhibited sexual passion, the conflict between Norma Jeane's desire for a career and Jim's insistence that she should remain an obedient housewife came to a head. There were quarrels but, as far as Jim was concerned, nothing was resolved. After he had returned to sea, however, Norma Jeane promptly went to Las Vegas (then a small hick town) to get her divorce. She returned to meet a build-up of requests for her modeling services and Emmeline suggested she changed

In 1946, at the age of twenty, Marilyn divorced her first husband, James E. Dougherty, and took her first screen test for Fox. She was also handling a busy career as a sought-after photographer's model.

her name to something which would look alright on the screen. She came up with "Jean Norman" which Norma Jeane didn't like, and it was soon dropped.

However, Emmeline had another trick up her sleeve. She composed a little publicity item and sent it off to the leading Hollywood gossip columnists Hedda Hopper and Louella Parsons. It read: "Howard Hughes must be on the road to recovery. He turned over in his iron lung and wanted to know more about Jean Norman, this month's cover girl on *Laff Magazine*."

This item was completely fabricated. At the time Hughes was recovering from severe injuries received in a plane crash and was certainly in no condition to read girlie magazines. But the item fueled Norma Jeane's ambitions, gave her some indication of what to do and how to do it. The first thing she did was to leave Ana Lower's place and to move in to the Studio Club, which sounds grand but which was little more than a hostel, run by studio executives' wives for young women wanting and waiting to get into the film industry.

In July 1946, the forty-five-year-old Ben Lyon was Head of Casting and New Talent at Twentieth Century Fox Pictures. He had been a film star himself for twenty years and had been the first person to spot the potential of Jean Harlow. It was into his office that Norma Jeane walked that afternoon, without an appointment. "It's Jean Harlow all over again," Lyon is alleged to have said. "She was absolutely gorgeous, dressed in a beautifully cut inexpensive cotton print and her golden hair down to her shoulders ...." After a short conversation he had signed her up for a seven-year optional contract and arranged a screen test in color – for her. This happened, it was seen later by the studio boss Darryl Zanuck who approved the contract.

Whether it was all as plain sailing as that we shall never know. Some sources claim that Lyon was already having an affair with Norma Jeane and trying to promote her film career (Lyon never confirmed or denied that rumor). Others suggest that the Howard Hughes paragraph had some influence. In any case, Lyon actually took several risks. He offered her a contract before a screen test, and he organized the test in color

which was against Twentieth Century Fox policy – he also persuaded the best photographers and make-up artists to prepare Norma Jeane for the test shoot.

He was also responsible for her name. He came up with several suggestions (including "Carol Lind") and then suddenly realized that Norma Jeane reminded him of the Broadway musical comedy actress Marilyn Miller – so why not Marilyn? Norma Jeane agreed but asked if she could use her grandmother's name – Monroe. They both agreed that it sounded fine, and the alliteration made it easy to remember.

The contract was a standard one. She would start at $75 a week, rising every six months by $25 to $150 a week reaching $1500 a week by the seventh year.

Jim Dougherty learned that his wife was divorcing him when he was in Shanghai, buying her a present. His first reaction was to cancel her allowance and when he returned home was unwilling to sign the divorce papers. Norma Jeane claimed that the divorce was just a career move and that she wanted to remain close. He rebelled at such demotion but eventually realized that the marriage now had no future and signed. Meanwhile, Gladys Baker, left alone in Ana Lower's house, asked to be returned to the state hospital.

Norma Jeane and all the people and places associated with her had finally gone. The stage was now set for the appearance of a new creature, a dazzling blonde called Marilyn Monroe.

As her fame grew as a much-in-demand model, somebody commented that this girl would look gorgeous even in a sack. Photographer Earl Theisen picked up the cue.

When the newly created Marilyn Monroe walked onto the Fox lot for her first day's work, Hollywood was at the height of its power and productivity and the notorious studio system was the norm. For anyone aspiring to be a film star – always very young and almost certainly penniless – signing a contract with a big studio would seem to be a marvelous beginning. It provided a regular income and access to all the essentials for a career – meeting directors, producers and studio executives, getting press coverage and a chance to learn the arts of film acting.

There were major traps, however, and when considering Marilyn Monroe's film career it is important to see what they were. One was income. Although an optional contract would include a raise every six months or so (and to a newcomer seem like riches), comparative to the amount of money a successful film could gross, the top salary after seven years would be peanuts. This was brought home savagely to Marilyn six years later when, as Hollywood's biggest box-office draw, she co-starred with Jane Russell in *Gentlemen Prefer Blondes*. Bound by a contract she was paid $18,000 for her work on the film which, after she had paid taxes and fees to her personal staff, did not amount to much. Russell, on the other hand, who was not bound by any contract, was paid $100,000.

The young starlets, of course, had no say in what sort of films they appeared in. At first, this may not have mattered – getting screen exposure was the essential thing. But once a potential star had become type-cast it was almost impossible to break out of the niche the studio had decided was hers. It took Marilyn many years and a great deal of pain to get rid of the "dumb blonde" image she was saddled with from the start.

That the young contract-players were exploited by the studios in other ways is undeniable. They were used as a free source of publicity for the studios, constantly doing pin-up or glamor portrait sessions (the press's appetite for star shots was insatiable), being told to open restaurants or shops, to make personal appearances at receptions, Hollywood parties, pageants and parades. Even when a young actress was actually working on a film these demands were maintained which added up to

long and exhausting days. Additionally, the youngsters had to find somewhere to live (preferably near the studio) and finance themselves – even to the clothes they wore for personal appearances. Suddenly the starting salary did not seem so very wonderful.

The studio would reply that the young players were being given a priceless training in film technique and unrivaled opportunities to make all-important contacts. But it was still a tough life and it needed toughness and determination to survive.

Marilyn was to prove that she possessed these qualities, but in 1946 she was a straightforward girl who believed that by doing the right thing she would succeed. From the beginning she plunged herself into studio life with enthusiasm. As we have seen, she had already developed a special relationship with the still camera and enjoyed the endless series of pin-up shots she was told to do. She took classes in acting, dancing and singing, made the requisite personal appearances. She became known around the Fox studios as a friendly but shy, enthusiastic and extremely pretty young starlet who, for some inexplicable reason, had not yet made it to the screen.

After the break-up of her marriage and before she became an established film actress, Marilyn made her living from modeling. One of her most regular patrons was magazine and calendar illustrator Earl Moran. "Earl saved my life many a time" Monroe once remarked about these hungry years. Of her, he simply said: "She is the sexiest." Photographs (facing page and overleaf) taken in his studio around 1946 by Moran were discovered in 1986 and reveal that, from her earliest years, Marilyn had no inhibitions about her naked body.

There is, in fact, a small mystery about which film Marilyn Monroe actually made her very first screen appearance in. Virtually all the biographies say it was the wierdly named *Scudda Hoo! Scudda Hay!*, which came up for her after she had been with the studio for six months. Sandra Shevey, in her book *The Marilyn Scandal* , says that she played walk-ons in two previous films – *The Shocking Miss Pilgrim* which starred Fox's reigning queen Betty Grable, and *You Were Meant for Me*, a vehicle for Jeanne Crain.

Scudda Hoo!, although featuring June Haver (another Fox blonde) and the young Natalie Wood, was a negligible teenage romp, instantly forgotten. But it did offer Marilyn a couple of small scenes. Both, however, ended up on the cutting-room floor and she was not listed in the credits. The sharp-eyed might catch a glimpse of her in a rowing boat at one point.

She was, however, given a credit in her next opportunity, *Dangerous Years*, a melodrama starring nobody in particular, about teenage delinquency. Marilyn played a waitress in a juke-box cafe, which allowed her a few attractive medium shots. When released, the movie sank without trace. Altogether, not a very propitious start, but even so Marilyn was shattered when, in August 1947, Fox refused to renew her contract and dropped her – before, incidentally, either of the films she participated in had been given a general release.

Depressed, but not destroyed, Marilyn survived by returning to her previous modeling career – and there was always plenty of work for her, both from camera artists and from painters like Earl Moran. By this time she had made one or two useful studio contacts and it was through the intervention of one of these, Joe Schenck, that in 1948 she was offered a contract with Columbia Studios. This led to her first really useful appearance on the screen, in a low-budget musical called *Ladies of the Chorus*. This film is important in Monroe's career partly because it gave her an opportunity to act, sing and dance, but also because it introduced her to two people who would have a great effect on her life.

Ladies of the Chorus concerns a burlesque chorus girl who falls in love with a rich socialite. The liaison is opposed by her mother (Adele Jurgens, also in the burlesque show) but of course all ends happily with a double wedding. Marilyn coped adequately with the demands this placed on her inexperience and actually received her first review. "One of the bright spots is Miss Monroe's singing," wrote the *Motion Picture Herald*. "She is pretty and, with her pleasing voice and style she shows promise." The song she delivered was "Everybody Needs a Da-Da-Daddy," one she would sing often over the years in personal appearances. Stills show her shining brightly, kicking her legs with the other sequinned ladies of the chorus, but with a slightly doll-like smile.

And then, once again, she was dropped by the studio. One version has it that the studio head Harry Cohn insisted that she could not act and never would. Another version suggests her dismissal was because she refused to spend a weekend alone with Cohen on his yacht.

After two years in the film business Marilyn Monroe had made two derisory films and a minor one, and she had been dropped by two major studios. Enough, surely, to suggest that she might more profitably try some other career. But by now she had made some good and important friends in the industry who encouraged her to hang on. One of these was her agent Harry Lipton, who knew that United Artists was looking for a very special sort of blonde for a spot in *Love Happy,* a film which was designed to revive the careers of the Marx Brothers, who had been absent from the screen for four years. He organized her an audition with Groucho (with whom she would play her one short scene) and got the role.

In the scene she merely had to rush into Groucho's office and say "Some men are following me," to which Groucho replies "I can't think why" – a line made hilarious by suggestive twitches of his famous eyebrows. This one short scene did a great deal for Marilyn – not least because it introduced the public to her sensational walk. She was also given an "Introducing Marilyn Monroe" on-screen credit. So people were asking who this girl was, and she was sent off to New York to promote the film which gave her a nice break from Hollywood and brought some valuable personal publicity.

Later that year she was back on the Fox lot playing a small part as a chorus girl in a pleasant enough stagecoach western called *A Ticket to Tomahawk*, starring Dan Dailey and Anne Baxter. She wore a short yellow dress with puff sleeves and trimmed with green bows. Her one song was called "Oh, What a Forward Young Man You Are" and she made next to no impact.

During 1949 two other important events occurred. After *Love Happy* she was out of work again and seemed to have no future in films. She managed to pick up a few modeling jobs and among the photographers who called her was Tom Kelley who, with his wife Natalie, got to know her quite well. This time he a very special assignment to interest her in.

The shot would be for a calendar and Marilyn would pose naked. She had no problems with nudity: the various people she lived with or shared apartments with at this time had got used to her spending much time naked. But she had turned down similar requests from other photographers. However her urgent need for cash, plus the fact she knew Kelley, persuaded her to. The results were some of the most famous pictures ever taken of Monroe. She is stretched languorously, gracefully across a rippling red velvet drape. The poses reveal her breasts, but otherwise are totally decorous. Even so, the post office considered the calendar pornographic and it was almost banned from the mails. Whether Marilyn considered what impact the nude posing might have on her career or reputation is unknown. She may have thought she had no film career at this point, she may have assumed she would not be recognized, she may just have felt it was something she could cope with if it ever came to a crisis. Eventually it did, and she coped admirably.

The second important event of 1949 was her meeting with one of the biggest and most important super-agents in the film industry. Johnny Hyde had met Marilyn casually once or twice over the years but only became really interested when he saw her short scene with Groucho Marx in *Love Happy*. Among the top

names he had handled were Lana Turner, Betty Hutton and Rita Hayworth. He was determined to create the same magic from this struggling young starlet.

Despite the ups and downs, three years in the Hollywood studios had done a great deal for Marilyn Monroe and it is probable that the experienced Hyde perceived in that one-minute scene in *Love Happy* qualities that had just not been there when he had met her previously. She had learned a lot and already had begun to surround herself with people able and willing to help her – professionally and emotionally.

One of her earliest and most powerful friends was Joseph Schenck, who founded Twentieth Century Productions in 1933 and was head of Twentieth Century Fox by 1935. In 1941 he served a prison sentence for perjury after bribing a labor racketeer, but by 1943 was back as head of productions at Fox. The story is that in 1947 he spotted the young Marilyn Monroe from his limousine as he was cruising across the Fox lot. He had his chauffeur stop and invited her for dinner. He was nearly seventy and she was twenty-one. She became a regular dinner guest over the years and clearly a strong friendship developed. That this included sexual favors is generally accepted (though Marilyn always denied it). Schenck did not wield much real power at this time but is thought responsible for getting her Columbia contract for *Ladies of the Chorus*, and for keeping a protective eye on her over the years.

Another benefactor in her early, hungry days was John Carroll, actor and singer who with his wife Lucille Ryman (then head talent scout and voice coach at MGM) took pity on her. Not only did they support her financially, but invited her to live with them. Some believe that Marilyn became Carroll's lover at this time and she certainly became very attached to him even asking Lucille if she would grant him a divorce. Lucille was very cool about this and after some emotional trials and tribulations Marilyn left the house and rented one of her own. This connection did however lead, a few years later, to one of Marilyn's major breakthroughs in film.

Despite her sensational figure and dazzling looks, it seems clear that this early stage of her

On the threshold of a career, Marilyn Monroe sits cross-legged in the center of a group of young contract players. Some would make it, some would not.

career few people were convinced that this young starlet had much acting talent. So when she arrived at Columbia for *Ladies of the Chorus* she was assigned coaches for both singing and acting. Both people were to have a profound effect.

Fred Karger was Columbia's vocal coach, handsome, thirty-two and recently divorced. Marilyn fell in love with him immediately and deeply and desperately wanted to marry him. Later she was always to refer to him as her first love. Karger, however, thought otherwise and did not consider her to be the right woman for him. He told her that her mind was not developed.

Having taken her on, Twentieth Century Fox preferred to promote more of a girl-next-door image for Monroe, as in these "baby-sitter" studies. The children were the twin sons of a studio worker, Roy Metzler, and at the time the shots were taken Monroe was working on her first official film Scudda Hoo, Scudda Hay! *(1948)*

The Kargers were an old Hollywood family. Fred's mother, Anne, attended both of Rudolf Valentino's weddings and their apartment was frequented by all the Hollywood greats of twenty or more years before. Marilyn and Anne established a strong, intimate bond which lasted until Monroe's death. When Ana Lower died in 1948, Anne Karger became Marilyn's prime female friend.

But perhaps the person who was to have the most powerful effect on Marilyn Monroe was Natasha Lytess. When they met in 1948, Lytess was Columbia's head drama coach and was asked to work specifically with Monroe, preparatory to *Ladies of the Chorus*. The two women struck up an instant accord and a very strong relationship developed which lasted for seven years. Lytess was certainly an excellent coach and nursed Monroe's talent with care and patience. But perhaps the most important thing she offered the young starlet was total faith in her talent. From the beginning she believed implicitly that Monroe had it in her to become a serious actress. Her belief was so strong that in 1950 Lytess gave up her job at Columbia to devote herself exclusively to Marilyn and sometime later the two women shared a home. There is a strong – but never thoroughly substantiated – rumor that there was a lesbian element in their relationship. This is probably based on a remark Monroe made: "She was a great teacher, but she got really jealous about the men I saw. She thought she was my husband." She certainly disliked Johnny Hyde and Joe DiMaggio.

Lytess exerted a profound effect on Marilyn and while making the ten movies which lie at the heart of her output, Monroe refused to do a single scene unless Natasha Lytess was on the set and could check out each take with her. This, naturally enough, infuriated her directors (apart from Billy Wilder) and was regarded as something as a joke by her fellow actors. The liaison was finally broken in 1956 when Marilyn found another, more prestigious coach in Paula Strasberg.

These people – the Carrolls, the Kargers, Schenck, Lytess, and Lipton acted as the fledgling star's support group. Emmeline Snively

In 1949 Monroe had been dropped by two studios and had no job. She returned to full-time modeling and posed nude for photographer Tom Kelley, who used the shots (facing page and overleaf) to create what became known as the Golden Dreams *calendar. When Monroe was on the way to becoming an established star three years later, the secret was revealed. Instead of trying to duck out, Monroe faced the press and scored one of the biggest publicity scoops in Hollywood history. The frivolous lace additions to one pose were added later to make the picture "decent" for wide distribution.*

Posed By **MARILYN MONROE**
In The Nude, With Lace Overprint

had started the transformation in 1945 and by the time Johnny Hyde came on the scene the outlines of what was to become the essential Marilyn must have been very evident: the celebrated walk was developing, she could dance and had proved she could do her own singing and her acting was in expert hands. Moreover, Lytess was introducing her to what one might call "culture" and Marilyn was determined to be not just a serious actress, but also a "complete person." To this end she was also attending private acting and mime classes and had begun to read, erratically but widely.

Hyde did a deal with Lipton and took over the representation of Marilyn. He equipped her with a new, glamorous wardrobe and made sure she was seen at every party, opening and nightclub. He was a short man, a complete gentleman, in his early fifties, just divorced, had a serious heart condition and fell totally in love with his new client.

It was a mirror-image of the Karger situation: Marilyn turned him down for the simple, basic reason that she did not love him. Hyde even asked Schenck to intervene on his behalf but even he got nowhere. It was becoming clear that Marilyn made a clear distinction between sex and love. She would go to bed with men she liked – but love meant marriage, and marriage meant love. A less scrupulous starlet might have jumped at the chance to marry Hyde and become respectable and rich at the same time.

In late 1949 the maverick film director John Huston was casting for a tough crime thriller, *The Asphalt Jungle*, about an aging criminal who, just released from prison, assembles a highly professional gang to carry out a million-dollar jewel theft. It was harsh, hard-boiled and would have an almost documentary feel to it. Louis Calhern was to play a corrupt lawyer who had a mistress, Angela (though the motion picture code restrictions insisted that she had to be called his niece!). This role was ideal for Marilyn, and Hyde did his utmost to get her an audition with Huston. There is a story that Lucille Ryman also leaned on Huston privately to secure the audition (he kept his race horses on the Ryman property without payment). Hyde recognized that this could be the big break he was looking

for. He requested a copy of the script so that Marilyn could go over it with Natasha and the pair of them escorted her to Metro Goldwyn Mayer where she read for Huston and landed the part.

During the shooting Monroe was obviously extremely nervous, but the support of fellow actors and the skillful direction of Huston got her through and the result achieved the impact that she and Johnny Hyde were hoping for. She made her mark in Hollywood itself, and for the first time the cinema-going public had a very clear idea who she was, and those who did not simply asked "Who's the blonde?" She began to be sought after by other producers. Hyde imagined he would have no problems negotiating a contract for her with Metro but the studio boss Dore Schary would not contemplate the idea.

Meanwhile Hyde found her a small part in a Mickey Rooney roller-skating epic called *The Fireball* (he wanted the public to see her as often as possible) which probably does not bear thinking about. Monroe was not pleased about this trivial movie, but in 1950 Hyde organized her a seven-year contract back at Twentieth Century Fox and, at last, her career began to accelerate. She was on the verge of the big breakthrough which would, in two years, make her Hollywood's biggest box-office draw and the world's favorite screen goddess.

With his ear ever to the ground, Hyde heard that Fox was preparing a new film written and directed by Joe Mankiewicz called *All about Eve*. In it there would be a small but important role which seemed ideal for Marilyn to follow up her success in *The Asphalt Jungle*. Mankiewicz recalled Hyde's persistence in securing the role for his client ("He haunted my office") and later how hard he fought those who resisted the idea of her returning to Fox.

As it turned out, *All about Eve* became one of the classics of American cinema – it is a backstage story about an ambitious young actress (Eve) who plots to unseat the star she is understudying (Margo Channing). Monroe plays Miss Caswell, the mistress of a waspish drama critic called Addison DeWitt, played by George Sanders. It has a witty, highly literate script and a

While in New York promoting her film Love Happy *(with the Marx Brothers) in 1949, Monroe did another photo session with Andre de Dienes, probably the best stills cameraman she ever worked with. These pictures were taken on Tobey Beach.*

The Asphalt Jungle (1950) was an important film in
Monroe's career. Her role was short, but she made a major
impact as the young mistress (above) of ageing gangster
Louis Calhern, and the public began to look for her name.

Although Marilyn Monroe made four films in 1950, the
studio kept her busy churning out pin-up photographs and
mindless publicity shots like this one (facing page), which
can only be described as a real turkey.

In All About Eve *(above)* Marilyn made the comparatively small role of theater critic George Sanders' mistress thoroughly memorable. With the two of them are Anne Baxter and Bette Davis.

Facing page: a publicity still from 1951. "The truth was that for all my lipstick, mascara and precocious curves, I was as unsensual as a fossil. But I seemed to affect people quite otherwise ..." said Marilyn looking back on her early years.

Facing page: this pin-up pose was actually released on Christmas Day, 1951, after it had been reported that Marilyn Monroe was "the present all GIs would like to find in their Christmas stocking." Below: Marilyn Monroe arrives at RKO radio studios to begin work on Clash by Night, *during which she attracted publicity attention away from her distinguished co-stars, Barbara Stanwyck and Paul Douglas.*

clutch of high-powered performances from Bette Davis (Margo), Anne Baxter (Eve), Celeste Holm, Thelma Ritter and Gary Merrill. The film won the Oscar as best picture, and Mankiewicz won the Oscar for best direction. Sanders won an Oscar as best supporting actor.

In fact Monroe was barely mentioned in the reviews, but following her appearance in *The Asphalt Jungle* this one certainly proclaimed the arrival of a star. But much to her distress, Hollywood seemed unable to take her seriously and refused to see her as more than a pushy, dumb blonde with no class. Even the people promoting her seemed to see her potential as that of a sex object rather than that of an actress.

A signed photograph, typical of the thousands that were sent out to fans every week. The amount of fan letters received by players was one way the studios had of assessing their success. Marilyn did very well.

Natasha Lytess continued her pressures and, although she and Johnny Hyde apparently hated each other, he must have picked up on Natasha's belief in Marilyn. About this time he began to talk to Metro chief Dore Schary about the possibility of Monroe playing Grushenka in a planned production of *The Brothers Karamazov*, from the novel by Dostoyevsky. The news of this leaked out to the press and one of the first major Marilyn Monroe jokes was born. The idea that this blonde bimbo should think herself able to tackle a heavy Russian classic was greeted with hoots of derision with the press asking insulting questions like "Which brother do you want to play?" (With hindsight it is safe to say that Monroe would have made a success of the project – certainly as good as, if not better, than Maria Schell who landed the role when the film was made eight years later.)

Depressed or not, Monroe continued working as hard as she could. She slipped in two quickies for Metro – *Right Cross*, in which she played Dick Powell's girlfriend and was not mentioned the credits, and *Hometown Story*, a propaganda film designed to boost American industry, in which Marilyn played a secretary. So, by the end of 1950 she had six films on release and was also recovering from plastic surgery that lifted her nose a fraction and gave her a stronger jawline.

Then two events occurred, one of which would have an immediate effect on her life though the impact of the other would have to wait a few years. In December 1950 Johnny Hyde died, his heart finally giving way under the strain. Marilyn went into a state of shock and there is a story, told by Lytess, that she made a suicide attempt at this point. Hyde's family and friends put a lot of distance between them and Marilyn and the William Morris Agency (for whom Hyde worked) was so cool she found a new agent, Hugh French.

In January of 1951 she had started work on *As Young as You Feel*, her first film for Fox under the new contract Hyde had organized. It was a Paddy Chayevsky story and starred Monty Woolley, Albert Dekker and Constance Bennett. Marilyn was cast (yet again) as a secretary. The film was the directorial debut of a protege of Elia Kazan called Harmon Jones.

Kazan visited the set one day, bringing with him his friend, the playwright Arthur Miller, who was in Hollywood trying to sell a screenplay. He and Marilyn got on extremely well and met again later at a private party. At first it seems she saw him as the father figure she had always lacked, but in talking to him she realized he was not grand or distant. Although Miller was thoroughly married at the time, a definite rapport grew up between them and they exchanged letters every so often. Marilyn told Natasha she was in love.

As Young As You Feel did Marilyn no harm. The film critic of the New York *Times* described her as "superb." At this stage in her career she was not yet pushing her sexual magnetism at the audience self-consciously, but rather working herself into her roles with insight and a developing sense of wit. A glimpse of the Marilyn to come was seen in her next project for Fox, *Love Nest*.

This neat little post-war story concerned a young man (William Lundigan) who returns home to his loving wife (June Haver) expecting a visit from an old army friend called Bobby. Monroe played Bobby – who was actually Roberta, a recently demobbed WAC. She was given a figure-hugging wardrobe and some provocative scenes but somehow her performance never seemed to take off. It has been suggested that this film prompted producers and directors to see that Monroe would always need strong support in her films since she seemed to sink or rise to the quality around her (Lundigan and Haver were low-key players).

In her next film, *Let's Make it Legal*, she certainly had stellar support with Claudette Colbert, Macdonald Carey and Zachary Scott as the top liners in a comedy about a grandmother (Colbert) about to be divorced and being courted by an old sweetheart. Monroe was cast as a voluptuous gold-digger. It was a brief part (which could have been played by any blonde) but as usual Marilyn brought her additional ability to handle laugh lines. By now cinema managers across the country were putting her name over the title of her films on their marquees, irrespective of her actual pecking order in the cast credits. And at last the chief

Clash by Night *was directed by Fritz Lang and Monroe supplied the "young love" interest, along with Keith Andes. She did quite a lot to promote blue jeans in this movie.*

"The trouble with censors is they worry if a girl has a cleavage. They ought to worry if she hasn't," Marilyn once remarked and, in this 1952 still, demonstrates exactly what she means.

Although it boasted an elite cast list, We're Not Married *(1952) stretched a mild joke well beyond its welcome. However, Marilyn was able to strut her stuff in a variety of swimming costumes and collected a deal of attention from the critics.*

executives at Fox were beginning to realize they had a real star on the payroll and, they told agent French, that is how they would handle her – no more trivial blonde bit parts. Moreover, other studios wanted to use her. RKO was after her for a film of Clifford Odet's play *Clash by Night*.

The publicity machine was in full action now. Every activity, appearance and detail about Monroe was grabbed by a world press hungry for news of this new sex queen. As always she was ever ready for a session with the stills camermen. She was adored by the public and the critics – and by people who considered cinema a popular art form. Accross the board, they were finding positive things to say about her performances. She was riding high, but the insecurities lurked underneath. She made an abortive attempt to contact Stanley Gifford, her father – and was cruelly rebuffed. And, ever eager to improve her acting, she began studying with Michael Chekhov, nephew of the Russian playwright and who had studied in Russia under Konstantin Stanislavsky.

1952 was to be a momentous year. She completed five films, survived two potential scandals, married her second husband and met the man who was to become her third.

Clash by Night was important for Monroe in several respects. She had been loaned out to RKO for the production, partly because Fox wanted as much exposure for her as possible at this time and also because the studio wanted to see how she would make out in a serious drama before they cast her in a psychological drama they had waiting for production. The film had a powerful cast – Barbara Stanwyck, Paul Douglas and Robert Ryan – and it was to be directed by the great German director of *Metropolis* and other films, Fritz Lang.

The story – full of sexual passion and jealousy – was removed from Clifford Odet's original setting of Staten Island to the cannery of a Californian fishing village. Monroe was to play Peggy, a young fun-loving cannery worker. Naturally, she was terrified – of Stanwyck (who had always terrified her on screen) of Paul Douglas (who hated her on sight) and most of all Lang who banned Lytess from the set when it

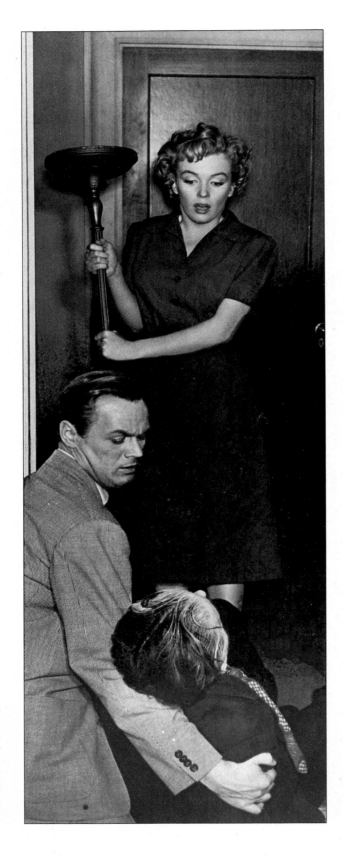

became clear that Monroe was relying on her rather than on the actual director. Moreover, her co-stars were alienated when the press and stills photographers concentrated more on Marilyn than on them. Paul Douglas is reported to have snarled: " Why the hell don't these goddam photographers ever take any pictures of us? It's only that goddam blonde bitch!" Apparently only Barbara Stanwyck could cool him off.

But, of course, she survived and attracted some good, serious notices. One critic wrote: "She is a forceful actress, too, when crisis comes along. She has definitely stamped herself as a gifted new star, worthy of all that press agentry ...." In 1982, Pauline Kael, the formidable film critic of the *New Yorker*, never a Monroe fan, wrote: "As a good-natured girl, full of animal high-spirits, Marilyn Monroe is appealing in an unmannered style that is very different from her later acting." Interesting, too, is the fact that this was the first film in which Monroe was acting in a natural setting – the beaches and coastal scenery of California. As later films would reveal she had a special relationship with natural landscapes, a quality seen in her first pin-up pictures taken in the Mojave desert by David

Despite her by now established fame as a sizzling blonde, Monroe was next cast as a psychotic baby-sitter in a drab little melodrama, Don't Bother to Knock *(these pages), which did nothing for her career. Her co-star was Richard Widmark who, understandably, looks worried.*

With Cary Grant during the filming of Monkey Business *(1952), which also involved a chimpanzee and the secret of eternal youth.*

Monroe arrives in New York on the promotion tour for Monkey Business. She was still generally known as "that blonde!" but this was practically the last film in which she would simply play a supporting role.

Conover and Andre de Diennes. And as a spin-off, she gave a tremendous boost to blue-jeans as sexy gear for a bright young woman. In those days the fashions that film stars wore were instantly copied in High Streets all over the western world. Marilyn set trends in several films of which this was the first.

Just before *Clash by Night* was due for release, producer Jerry Wald received an anonymous telephone call from a man claiming that he had proof Marilyn had posed for a nude calendar which was hanging up in bars and garages all over the country. In a pathetic blackmail attempt he demanded $10,000 to keep quiet.

The studio executives went into a panic and urged Monroe to deny the charge, to reject the suggestion that she would ever do anything so awful as pose in the nude. But Monroe refused. It is clear that she had a far better estimate of her relationship with her public than the film executives did. Eventually the story was handed to a wire service reporter Aline Mosby. In her report she emphasized Marilyn's deprived orphanage background, her foster homes, her unsuccessful marriage. She only did the pictures because she was hard up, "a week behind with my rent ..." (which was true). She knew that the public would be touched by her frank admission of "honest poverty" – and they were. She had achieved one of the biggest publicity scoops in film history.

The second potential scandal of that year was less easy to negotiate, but once more Marilyn came out unscathed. Late in 1952 a journalist

In O'Henry's Full House *(facing page) (1952) Marilyn played a classy streetwalker in an episode which also featured Charles Laughton as a tramp. Right:* Niagara *(1953) was created specifically to launch Marilyn Monroe as a major star. "It is as if everything she had done prior to 1952 had been done in preparation for* Niagara. *The half-lidded gaze; the moist, painted, parted lips; the artificially blonde hair; and the low, husky, breathy voice – it's all here" (Randall Riese and Neil Hitchens).*

discovered Marilyn's mother, Gladys Baker, living in a state mental hospital. This was decidedly awkward. A studio biography, issued by Fox in February 1951, placed great emphasis on her childhood in the orphanage and foster homes and as a ward of the state: " Her mother was a helpless invalid and her father was killed in an automobile accident shortly after her birth. Marilyn has never known either ...."

The new revelation would mean a deconstruction of this story and once again there was a temptation to lie. But once again the studio publicists risked telling the truth – or, at least, an economical version of the truth. A statement was issued: "Unbeknown to me as a child, my mother spent many years as an invalid

Niagara *(these pages)* is *"the only movie that explored the mean, unsavory potential of Marilyn Monroe's cuddly, infantile perversity. There's no affection for her here ..."* *(Pauline Kael).*

In Niagara *(these pages) Monroe plays Rose Loomis, a frustrated wife on holiday with her war-shocked husband, Joseph Cotton. She has another man in view and plans murder. Henry Hathaway directed and, by general agreement, did a sensational job on highlighting his star's assets. Even the falls took second place.*

in a state hospital ... I haven't known my mother intimately, but since I have become grown and able to help her, I have contacted her." Curiously this evasive and unconvincing statement was accepted by press and public. A month later Gladys was transferred from the state to a luxurious private nursing home the fees for which Marilyn could now afford.

Marilyn, it seemed, could get away with anything now. One thing she did not get away with during this eventful year, was her second marriage. The man involved was Robert Slatzer who met Monroe in the summer of 1946 when she was a struggling starlet and he was a struggling show-business journalist. They formed a steady friendship which lasted over the years of Marilyn's climb to stardom.

Their marriage is alleged to have taken place at Tijuana, Mexico in October 1952. But the union was dissolved three days later at the insistence of Darryl F. Zanuck, Marilyn's boss at Twentieth Century Fox. Some Marilyn observers find it difficult to believe that this marriage took place, but Sandra Shevey asserts in the Los Angeles *Herald Examiner* that documentation exists. Slatzer told Shevey that he and Marilyn were summoned to Zanuck's office where he said: "We have spent half a million dollars promoting Marilyn's image as the Ideal Girl waiting for Mister Right to have kids. If it gets out that she is married and no longer accessible, her fan mail will drop ... we are contemplating whether to renew her option. I do not want this marriage to last."

If her studio was trying to suggest that 1953 was all fireworks (facing page) for Marilyn Monroe, then it was correct. Niagara *was a world-wide sensation and her most quintessential film –* Gentlemen Prefer Blondes *– was about to appear. After her series of roles as assorted psychotics and subservient secretaries,* Gentlemen Prefer Blondes *(right) at last defined the actress Monroe would become, demonstrating her sexy innocence, her unerring comic flair and her song-and-dance abilities.*

In 1953 the "mean, moody and magnificent" Jane Russell was an established glamor star. To team her with Monroe for Gentlemen Prefer Blondes (these pages) was a brilliant stroke – they are perfect foils for each other in both the dramatic and the musical scenes.

The success of Gentlemen Prefer Blondes *put Monroe on top. In her next film* How To Marry a Millionaire (these pages) *she acted alongside Lauren Bacall and Betty Grable, playing three girls out to trap a millionaire each. After this film, Grable had been toppled as Fox's top blonde.*

At that time Marilyn did not have the heft to stand up to the studio's edict so the marriage was annulled. Sentimentalists claim she thus sacrificed her one chance of a committed, stable relationship for the sake of her career since she was about to make the film which would turn her into an international star. Not for the first time – and certainly not for the last – Marilyn's film career came before anything else.

Apart from *Clash by Night* there were four other films released in 1952. Three of them were fairly ordinary and did not really extend Monroe's abilities very much, though she was getting more show-casing and exposure. *We're Not Married* was a five-episode film about five couples, all married by the same justice of the peace, who discover two years later that his license was not valid at the time. Monroe had stiff competition in this movie – the other wives were played by Ginger Rogers, Eve Arden, Mitzi Gaynor and Zsa Zsa Gabor – but she made her mark as the beauty queen who, finding she can not now enter the Miss America competition, enters the Miss Mississippi contest instead. Silly, but fun. She was also given a slot in another omnibus film *Full House*, derived from four short stories by O. Henry. Marilyn played an elegant street walker who is accosted by an equally well-dressed down-and-out played by the formidable Charles Laughton. *Monkey Business* found her in yet another inane comedy, playing with Cary Grant and Ginger Rogers.

Far more interesting was Fox's decision to cast her in a psychological drama *Don't Bother to Knock*. Monroe fans do not like this one. It is a tight little piece set in real time and we find Marilyn as a psychotic baby-sitter in a New York hotel. She fantasizes about being rich and beautiful, entices a man (Richard Widmark) into her room, makes a murderous attempt on the child and is only just prevented from making one on herself. The film has been called "a slow-moving and melodramatic bore," but Pauline Kael writes: "[Marilyn Monroe's] unformed – almost blobby – quality is very creepy, and she dominated this melodrama."

In fact, she did receive some rather poor notices, but it was the first film she made in which she was unequivocally the star. Anne Bancroft, who was also in the movie (her Hollywood first) said "It was so real, I responded, I really reacted to her. She moved me so that tears came into my eyes ...." Monroe herself always believed that this film contained her best dramatic acting and yet both the critics and Fox executives felt that she was out of her depth.

Nevertheless she was then cast in another thriller, the film which would launch her on the world as a fully-fledged megastar in her own right – *Niagara*. After this film anything she had done previously was forgotten, all the dumb blonde parts, the secretaries and walk-ons. But 1952 had already dropped another bombshell on her. One evening in March that year a girlfriend called her to arrange an evening out at a Hollywood restaurant. She tried to get out of it but finally agreed to go and found herself having dinner with Joe DiMaggio, a retired baseball player of whom Marilyn had never heard.

Marilyn at her most memorable and incandescent: the "Diamonds are a Girl's Best Friend" number from Gentlemen Prefer Blondes. *Eventually the public would prefer some of her later films, but this was the clip every television channel showed when her death was announced in 1962.*

Marilyn Monroe and Joe DiMaggio did not commit themselves to marriage until January 1954, but he was an integral part of her life almost from the moment they met in March 1952. This was, in effect, a blind date. Apparently DiMaggio had seen a photograph of Monroe – not a film still, but a publicity glamor shot with members of the Chicago White Sox. He asked a friend to set up a foursome date.

Marilyn knew nothing of baseball and had only the vaguest idea who DiMaggio was. She was prejudiced against ball players, expecting them to be loud and flashy. DiMaggio was neither. He wore an immaculate, conservative suit, had a touch of grey in his hair, was reticent and polite. Although Marilyn drove him back to his hotel after the first date she refused his invitation to come inside and he rang her daily for two weeks without result. But Marilyn, impressed, had been doing her homework and learned enough about him to become interested in calling him for a date, after which they became inseparable.

Joseph Paul DiMaggio was born in California in 1914. He began his career as a ball player with the New York Yankees in 1936. In 1941, after the Yankees had lost four games in a row DiMaggio broke the modern major-league record for consecutive hits with a fifty-six game streak, and he led his team into ten World Series championships. Known as "Joltin' Joe" and "the Yankee Clipper" he went into the record books as the greatest baseball player of them all, retiring in 1951 when he was earning $100,000 a year – the first ball player in history to receive such a salary. He had married an actress, Dorothy Arnold, but that ended in divorce, and his son, Joe Jr., was in his early teens and about to go off to military school.

Joe was living happily in San Francisco where his sister Marie kept house and he owned a restaurant on Fisherman's Wharf, a favorite tourist haunt. He was not a particularly sociable man, preferring evenings at home with his male friends talking sport, or watching television. He did not dance and disliked parties, and he was at his happiest fishing from his boat. In many ways he seems the least likely partner for a brash, glamorous film star.

But the public was enchanted. From the outside at least they seemed the perfect match – America's favorite blonde and America's favorite sportsman. It seems clear that despite their evident differences, Joe and Marilyn were making a serious effort to create a satisfactory relationship. In many ways he represented the kind of man Marilyn had always been drawn to from the days of her marriage to Jim Dougherty – big, gentle, conservative, masculine and a brilliant lover. And they were certainly in love. But basic differences began, with increasing frequency, to rock their boat. He hated Hollywood and the whole film industry with which Marilyn was surrounded; he was particularly impatient with her friends and professional colleagues whom he contemptuously called "phonies." He especially hated Natasha Lytess.

Marilyn Monroe and Joe DiMaggio enjoyed a stormy but on-going relationship for more than a year before they actually married. Although he did not approve of her cinema career, he willingly accompanied her to Banff in Alberta, Canada, for her location work on River of No Return. *He knew there was good fishing in the area.*

They tried living together – he had clothes at her place, she had clothes at his. She met his family and – to Joe's delight – started an instant rapport with his son, who was to remain a loyal and close friend right up to the day of her death. But as their courtship developed and their affair intensified over eighteen months, DiMaggio's views on Marilyn's career itself became evident. He disliked the roles she had been playing and hated the low-cut, clinging dresses she wore on and off screen. While they were together it was remarked that Marilyn was tending to dress more discreetly. Certainly the public and the press speculated that, having found such a splendid catch, Marilyn would retire from the screen. But whenever she was asked about this, Marilyn would absolutely deny she any intention of retiring.

It is possible to see DiMaggio's point of view, the assumptions he might have made. When they met his fame was greater than hers, and her fame was mostly hype, in any event quite disproportionate the quality of the films she had been involved in up to that point. He wanted a beautiful, sexually compatible wife with whom he could settle down quietly and maybe thought he offered a preferable alternative to appearing in a succession of second-rate, forgettable movies. And maybe, especially after the death of Johnny Hyde and the mostly indifferent reviews she received for *Don't Bother to Knock* , the thought may have crossed Marilyn's mind. But such a plan was given no time for consideration, let alone take root, because while they were discussing whether to go for marriage, Marilyn

In River of No Return *Marilyn had to do some arduous location work (facing page), but the finished film did not seem to justify the struggle. Her co-star was Robert Mitchum. Right: a publicity shot from around the time of* River of No Return.

was cast in the film which really would make her an absolute star and catapult her into worldwide fame.

For hard core Monroe fans, *Niagara* is a cult movie. This is (partly at least) because it is so bad – an unlikely melodrama that gives up on psychology half way through and resorts to unlikely plot twists and an affair with the big waterfall. However, it does contain some classic Monroe moments.

She plays Rose Loomis, a young wife visiting the celebrated honeymoon spot with her impotent husband recently released from a mental institution. She plans to murder him and run off with her young lover. Wrote Pauline Kael: "This isn't a good movie but it's compellingly tawdry and nasty – the only movie

Above: Monroe and DiMaggio were married on January 14, 1954, at San Francisco City Hall. She wore a chocolate brown suit with an ermine collar. He wore the polka-dot tie he had been wearing the first time he met her.

While Marilyn and DiMaggio were on a wedding trip in Japan she agreed to take time off to visit and entertain the American troops (previous page and these pages) in Korea. Later, Monroe was to describe this tour as one of the high spots of her career. Servicemen traveled from all parts of the Korean peninsula to see her and she, in turn, responded to their spontaneous affection with warmth.

Monroe gave several
open-air
performances in
Korea. Even though
the wind was icy and
there were flurries of
snow, she changed
into a low-cut, plum-
colored, sequinned
dress to give them her
sexiest songs –
including "Diamonds
are a Girl's Best
Friend."

The most admired couple in America, soon after their marriage. Joe disapproved of his wife's career and he also disapproved of the low-cut, revealing dresses she wore – hence, presumably, the strategically placed rose in this picture. Facing page: Marilyn in New York in 1954.

that explored the mean, unsavoury potential of Marilyn Monroe's cuddly, infantile perversity."

The film's most famous scene is one long take when the camera simply follows Monroe as she walks, in high heels and a skin-tight dress, 150 feet along a cobblestone path, the lens transfixed by her wide-swinging bottom. Theoretically the ultimate in vulgarity, but everyone agrees Monroe transcended that through her grace and the way she seems completely at ease with her own body. She was also allowed to sing (a song called "Kiss") and there were several other steamily erotic scenes for her. This film represents Monroe as the studio's idea of the ultimate sex object and showed the public the final transformation from Norma Jeane into sex goddess.

It was not just her body and the way she handled it; her voice had dropped to a sexually-charged huskiness, her mouth was moist and slightly open (Pauline Kael later found similarities between her and the pop singer Mick Jagger), and finally her hair was now at its blondest. All this was due to her loyal team, including Natasha Lytess and Whitey Snyder, her make-up man. Director Henry Hathaway and cinematographer Joe MacDonald made the most of the opportunities offered – never before, and probably never afterwards, had Marilyn been photographed so superbly.

The film was an instant worldwide hit. It was also one of the sexiest movies to emerge from Hollywood since the Hays Office forced the codes of decency on the industry, and it almost

In the summer of 1954, Marilyn had just completed her work on the Irving Berlin musical There's No Business Like Showbusiness *and then went on, without a break, to make* The Seven Year Itch. *Here she is caught by the studio cameraman at this time.*

An off-set production still from There's No Business Like Showbusiness *with Donald O'Connor. This splashy musical gave her little to do as a nightclub singer trying to marry into an established show-business family.*

In The Seven Year Itch *(these pages) Marilyn plays a sexy model living upstairs from a married man whose wife is away. The film revealed, yet again, her great talent for comedy. Tom Ewell shared the acting honors. Above: veteran comic Victor Moore had a cameo role as the plumber who releases Marilyn's toe from the bath tap.*

created the start of another purity campaign.

Although Joe DiMaggio had disapproved of Marilyn playing a street walker in O. Henry's *Full House*, he seems to have kept his thoughts about *Niagara* to himself. He had accompanied Marilyn east and they had enjoyed a brief break in New York where Joe had friends. Director Hathaway had been prepared for Marilyn to be difficult in the set – she was already getting a reputation for fluffing lines and relying on her coach. In the event, apparently, she was no trouble at all. Later Hathaway commented: "Joe was there to keep her happy."

Niagara was released in January 1953, immediately broke all records and Marilyn was now among the top-grossing stars. An incident which happened at this time gives some

indication of the kind of sensation she was creating. The magazine *Photoplay* awarded her its prestigious Gold Medal as the best new star of the year. It was presented at a splendid ceremony at the Beverly Hills Hotel and attended by all the industry's top brass and, of course, other stars. Marilyn appeared, late, sewn into gold lame with a magnificent cleavage. As she hobbled to receive her award the males in the audience started whistling and hooting and Jerry Lewis (the comedian and master of ceremonies) leaped onto a table and began pawing the tablecloth.

Joan Crawford was present and, using her authority as Hollywood aristocracy, attacked Marilyn in a magazine interview: "The publicity

The most famous scene in The Seven Year Itch *(these pages) is when a blast of air from the subway blows Marilyn's skirt high around her – in fact, this is possibly the most enduring of all the Monroe images. The filming of it did not please DiMaggio and is likely to have been the last straw that broke this already fragile marriage.*

Though there is no record of Monroe being particularly superstitious, she had her palm read by Hassan, a fortune teller working at the Beverly Hills Hotel.

has gone too far, and apparently Miss Monroe is making the mistake of believing her own publicity ...." When the mortified Marilyn was asked for a comment, her reply seems a touch oblique: "I've always admired her for being such a wonderful mother," she said, "for taking four children and giving them a fine home ...." At the time, rumors that Crawford was anything but a good mother were rife and Marilyn would certainly have heard them. What DiMaggio had to say about the incident is not recorded.

With *Niagara* following *Don't Bother to Knock*, Marilyn could quite easily have become type-cast, not as a dumb blonde but as a psychotic blonde (and may well eventually have attracted the attention of Hitchcock). But for her next film Fox, with what seemed like utter perversity, cast her in a big musical *Gentlemen Prefer Blondes*. Or perhaps it was intended to be a reminder that she was just a dumb blonde after all. For Lorelei Lee, the creation of novelist Anita Loos in the 1920s, is probably the most naive and witless blonde ever invented. In the Broadway musical version Carol Channing got away with it by caricaturing the part. Marilyn played it straight, but with her newly acquired poise, rapidly developing sense of timing and ability to mine dialogue for laughs, created something entirely different. Then there was the singing and the dancing, aspects of her talent which had hardly been exploited at all in her previous films. Studio boss Darryl Zanuck apparently did not even know she could sing.

As Lorelei's friend, Dorothy, the studio

brought in Jane Russell who, at that time, was Hollywood's other reigning bombshell – her breasts and Marilyn's bottom were intended to ignite audiences all over the world. If Monroe seemed ethereal, Russell was brunette and earthy. It was a superb combination.

For this film Marilyn had a taste of true stardom by getting her own luxurious dressing room. However, it was often difficult to get her out of it. A neurotic conviction that she was not good enough to do what was required of her was beginning to grow. She was also being labeled a workaholic and this pattern would be repeated in all her subsequent films. She would arrive hours before she was required and would often stay on longer, rehearsing. But getting her in front of a camera was the problem. In this film, too, she met another important colleague – Jack Cole, the choreographer. After *Gentlemen Prefer Blondes* she would never do a dance routine in any film unless Cole worked it out for her. Although she had a natural talent for singing, she was no dancer. But with Cole she was willing to work into the night to get it right. His work for her in the show-stopping *Diamonds Are a Girl's Best Friend* sequence justifies her faith (and his talent). It is the most quintessential footage from all of Monroe's movies and the one all television stations showed on the day her death was announced. "Never on film has she been so much the mistress of a situation. Marilyn comes across in this number as positively luminous," writes Fred Lawrence Guiles.

As early as this rumors started that DiMaggio and Monroe were having occasional fights, mainly about her screen roles and the revealing costumes she was wearing. But he was still bombarding her with roses, they were still living in a haze of sexual pleasure and trying to avoid talking about things which might escalate into arguments which would threaten the fragile relationship they were trying to strengthen.

When Monroe first walked onto the Fox lot in 1946, the studio's biggest star was Betty Grable; she was the highest paid woman in the country and during the war had been the soldiers' favorite pin-up. This no doubt helped her to remain among the top ten box-office stars for

thirteen years – longer than any other actress in films. She was cast alongside Marilyn in the next Fox picture *How to Marry a Millionaire* . The story, written by Nunnally Johnson, was about three gold-digging girls chasing rich men in New York. The third woman was to be played by Lauren Bacall. The film was made in the new Cinemascope process.

The movie was well-received, as a light comedy with many critics making obvious remarks about Monroe being stretched across the huge wide screen. The most memorable feature of her role as Polo, was that she was near-sighted and could not see a thing without her glasses. A pretty crude device but one which Marilyn exploited deliciously. She was still working on her acting with Michael Chekhov, who helped her prepare her lines for the film. She also began taking lessons in mime and movement from Lotte Goslar, a talented and distinguished teacher; and their work showed. One critic commented: "Her stint as a deadpan comedienne is as nifty as her looks," and another remarked: "It is particularly noteworthy that Miss Monroe has developed more than a small amount of comedy polish ...."

Of course, everybody was waiting to see what would happen when the established star (Grable) met the new star. But instead of sparks flying the two women got on very well. All the problems which would make filming such an agony for her were not evident in Monroe's studio behavior – lateness, fluffing lines, reliance on her coach, complete insecurity. However, Lauren Bacall has mentioned that she started drinking too much.

But Grable seems to have gone out of her way to be kind, helpful and even nurturing. Two films later Betty Grable retired from filmmaking and Monroe inherited her dressing-room. Today, *How to Marry a Millionaire* seems stilted and dated, mainly because our perceptions of the relationship between men and women has changed so radically, but it contains some nice Monroe moments – and it was beautifully costumed.

After two artificial, sophisticated comedies her next film asked her to return to realistic drama, and a western at that. This was *River of No*

Although the couple
were in mid-divorce,
Joe DiMaggio
accompanied Monroe
to the premier of The
Seven Year Itch on
June 1st, 1955. The
divorce was granted
a few days later and
their marriage of less
than two years was
over.

Return , to be directed by the formidable Otto Preminger and would co-star Robert Mitchum (her first husband's buddy in the Lockheed factory days). Marilyn was to play a saloon singer who befriends a small boy whose father has been serving a prison sentence for shooting a man. There were opportunities for her to sing, some good action stuff on the river; and this was the first of Monroe's films which suggested that the great outdoors made the most marvelous setting for her particular kind of vulnerability.

But before the filming was completed she made perhaps the most dramatic move of her life. Despite the runaway success of her last two films, there were many discontents connected with her career. She still felt she was not being taken as seriously as she should be, both off-stage (the Crawford incident, for example) and on (the dumb blonde roles). Moreover, Fox was keeping her to her seven-year contract with its greatly restricted income (she was getting less per picture than her co-stars – Russell and Grable – even when she so obviously wiped them off the screen). DiMaggio was still pressuring her to let go of her career and it is possible she reasoned that if Hollywood could be persuaded to take her seriously and develop her in the kind of films she really wanted, then Joe would perhaps view her career in a more tolerant light.

A solution presented itself unexpectedly in the late summer of 1953 when she had a photo session with a visiting New York fashion photographer Milton Greene. At thirty-one he was a slight, handsome young man and already a brilliant photographer. He and Marilyn got on immediately. When they met she is reported to have remarked "Why, you're just a boy," to which he replied "And you're just a girl." How they came finally to draw up the plan is not known, but she unloaded all her problems on Greene who decided his mission was to "rescue" her from Hollywood. Although he had no experience in the movie industry, he persuaded a Wall Street backer to partner him in an independent film company with Marilyn.

Called Marilyn Monroe Productions, the company would give her all she needed – script control, director approval and more money. Today the independent producer is the norm in filmmaking; actors write and direct, as well as produce films. But in 1953 such a move had never been heard of since Charlie Chaplin, Mary Pickford and Douglas Fairbanks started United Artists. From this point of view Monroe can be credited with a movie history first. For the time being, however, she kept quiet about this move and got on with *River of No Return* .

Filming became the usual story of a Monroe epic: Natasha Lytess created problems and was banned from the set by Preminger, Marilyn had an accident in one of the action sequences and sprained her ankle; and she, who adored children, was shattered to learn that ten-year-old Tommy Rettig consulted a priest about the advisability of working with "a woman like her." A consolation was the presence of DiMaggio and some of his cronies – they were attracted by the fishing potential at the film's location – Banff in Alberta, Canada. "Joe was very nice and a good influence on Marilyn," Preminger recalls. Joe also thawed young Rettig to an extent by taking him fishing.

It remains something of a mystery exactly why Monroe finally agreed to marry DiMaggio.

She committed herself in November 1953 and fixed the date for January of the following year. The main issue between them had always been as to whether she would continue her career. It is possible that knowing she was on the verge of going into independent production had given her confidence, believing that Joe would raise fewer objections if he realized she was in control of her life. She had already thrown down a challenge to Fox.

The studio wanted to cast her in in a film to be called *The Girl in Pink Tights* , actually a re-make of an old Grable vehicle, co-starring her with Frank Sinatra. But she refused to do it, declaring that the script was lousy and fearing that, once more, the studio would feature her as a blonde in pink tights. Even the presence of Sinatra, with whom she was friendly and was later to have an affair, was not bait enough. So the studio suspended her.

A week later she married DiMaggio. It was a big media event and the couple honeymooned in a friend's mountain lodge near Palm Springs. It seems to have been a happy time at first –

possibly because, being suspended, there was no film immediately demanding her attention. However, the wheels were turning. The Fox executives, not really wanting to lose their major star, made a conciliatory gesture and restored her to the payroll, shelving the *Pink Tights* project. They refused, however, to give her script approval.

After the honeymoon the DiMaggios returned to San Francisco and settled down again with Joe's sister Marie running the household. It was a brief, quiet time. Joe Jr. came home from school and instantly got on with his new stepmother. Then in April the couple left for Japan.

Although this was basically a business baseball trip for Joe it almost accidentally produced what Marilyn would always look upon as one of the major highlights of her career. The couple was feted outrageously in Tokyo (both were idolized in that country) and at a reception Marilyn was approached by a U.S. Army officer who asked her if she would consider making a quick trip to visit the soldiers in Korea. Although Joe was not pleased, Marilyn leaped at the chance and in four days did ten live shows for more than one hundred thousand troops. In a tight, low-cut sequinned dress she stood on open-air stages in the biting winds with flurries of snow, and delivered her best-known numbers from *Blondes*, and also "Do It Again" which was considered too risque for the troops. Her voice was small, but the field amplification was effective enough for her songs to carry. The men went crazy, and back home army discipline was called into question. But that was the only criticism; the press adored the trip – for once, a film star had made a tremendous gesture on her own and performed it in her own time. Never before had the world press been so pro-Marilyn Monroe.

For her, the impact of performing live – especially under such circumstances – was profound. In the hothouse atmosphere of Hollywood she only knew her fans through their letters and box-office takings. Here she was face to face with the real thing and she wallowed in it. Her fragile sense of confidence was given a tremendous boost. But she returned from the trip with mild pneumonia and was out of action for a

few days before she and Joe concluded their tour of Japan.

Back in San Francisco it became clear that Marilyn was expected to subside into a dutiful, quiet wife while Joe returned to his bachelor habits of evenings with his cronies. Having no domestic skills and little in common with the tightly-knit members of Joe's large Italian family, Marilyn must have quickly felt redundant and bored.

When Fox sent her the script of a film called *There's No Business Like Showbusiness* she accepted at once even though it was definitely an inferior piece of work. Some have speculated that she would have done anything to get out of the DiMaggio household. Others suggest she took it on because she she was anxious to secure *The Seven Year Itch* as her next project.

Curiously the two worst films of Marilyn's days of stardom are both musicals. *There's No Business Like Showbusiness* proposes a story about a family of troopers, with Monroe cast as a scheming night-club singer who disrupts family unity. This unoriginal plot is simply a device to string together a lot of old Irving Berlin songs and also to employ a bunch of musical stars Fox had under contract – Ethel Merman, Dan Dailey, Mitzi Gaynor, Donald O'Connor and the current pop star, "crying" Johnny Ray. Nothing works. Merman was never a screen performer, the others repeated old tricks and even Marilyn's innate taste deserted her. Her three solo numbers are simply tacky.

It is not surprising that DiMaggio objected to her participation in this film. Together they were a major publicity item but when he visited the set he refused to be photographed with his wife. He did agree, however, to pose with Ethel Merman who, to him, represented a lifetime of hard work and the "respectability" of Broadway (where she had been the reigning musical star for more than twenty years). Filming was painful as usual. Monroe collapsed on the set several times, there were fights with Joe. It was a film that did no good for anyone.

No sooner was work on the musical completed, than Marilyn was rushed straight into *The Seven Year Itch* , which had been a highly successful Broadway play starring Tom Ewell

(who would repeat his role in the film). In it he plays a "summer bachelor," a married man whose wife and family have sought cooler climes while he must remain working through a sweltering summer in New York. Monroe is the girl upstairs with whom he starts a relationship which is mostly fantasy.

It is an important film in Monroe's career because it gave her an opportunity to humanize the blonde image that the studios had so far created. She was, at last, playing nearer to her real self (as all great comedians do) than in the plastic, predictable and patronizing blonde gold-diggers she had tackled before. This ability would never leave her now. Formula acting was in the past and she would illuminate every

Marilyn enjoyed her Hollywood social life. At a nightclub here, her companions are (from left) the young Lithuanian beefcake actor Jacques Sernas, entertainer Sammy Davis Jnr., Milton Greene (with whom she would form her own production company) and singer Mel Torme.

For a while Marlon Brando was a regular Monroe escort.

subsequent film with her own infinitely touching quality. .

Filming went without a hitch. Billy Wilder directed and reportedly found no problems with the omnipresent Lytess ("I regarded the coaches as my co-workers" he said). The chemistry between Ewell and Monroe worked beautifully – they both come across as slightly weird and spaced-out and, for once, she did not run off with the whole film.

DiMaggio, however, was opposed to the project from the start. Their relationship was already foundering badly, there were many quarrels mostly focusing on what she was doing on the screen. It is as if DiMaggio could not see Marilyn as an actress doing a job, but only as his wife doing things deliberately to insult him as a man and a husband. One of these "insults" would become a highlight of the movie and a Monroe classic image for ever.

As the relationship between Ewell and Monroe progresses he takes her to the pictures. When they come out of the cinema into this steamy hot New York night she steps onto a subway grating and a train passing below sends an airstream which blows her wide, white pleated skirt high above her thighs.

Wilder set this scene up in New York and started filming it just after midnight. Even so huge crowds collected to watch and at every take they cheered with delight and some of the males there resorted to the kind of hoots and catcalls which had humiliated Monroe at the *Photoplay* awards. DiMaggio was there, too. Unwisely he had followed Monroe to New York and lurked on the fringes of the spectators, scowling and angry.

Marilyn finished her session at 4.15 a.m. and returned to the St. Regis Hotel where she and Joe were staying. The rest of the night the hotel guests overheared shouting, scuffling and hysterical crying. One guest placed a complaint at reception. The following morning DiMaggio checked out and returned to California. The marriage was at an end after nine months.

The skirt-billowing scene was obviously not the reason for the separation, but it probably represented the last straw for both of them. DiMaggio saw it as a humiliation to himself as her husband, she saw it as just a part of her job. But the relationship had become increasingly stormy – some commentators claim that Joe would use violence and slap Marilyn around a bit.

The official separation happened in early October. Reporters were told that it was because of their "incompatability resulting from the conflicting demands of their careers."

To celebrate the completion of *The Seven Year Itch*, its producer, Charlie Feldman, hosted a magnificent dinner party for Marilyn at Romanoff's. All Hollywood royalty (executives and stars) turned out. Marilyn danced with her life-long hero Clark Gable and Fox head Zanuck told her that she was "incredibly good" in the new movie. She was at the peak of her personal and professional achievement, but the next film she was offered was a trashy piece called *How to be Very, Very Popular*, which she promptly turned down – and then disappeared.

Although the press made a meal of this ("Where is Marilyn?"), she had actually gone to stay with her old friend Anne Karger while she tried to settle her differences with Fox. But ten days later she packed up, flew east and went to stay with Milton Greene and his wife Amy who, with their small son Josh had a country place in New England and an apartment in New York.

This was more than a brief escape from Hollywood; it was a definite decision to try and alter her life. She was putting the studio system behind her, Greene was working hard to get their production company off the ground, and New York also represented a more serious approach to art and acting to which she had been aspiring for so long. There was another attraction – Arthur Miller.

Marilyn loved the country, walking the Greene's dogs and occasionally babysitting with Josh. It all helped in her recovery from both the hassles of Hollywood and the emotional traumas associated with Joe DiMaggio. She loved New York, too, and eventually moved there to live at the Waldorf-Astoria Hotel before getting her own apartment in exclusive Sutton Place, overlooking the East River. For a while she studied acting with the veteran actress Constance Collier who thought Marilyn could be "the most exquisite Ophelia" – and her friend Greta Garbo agreed. But Miss Collier died later that year and soon afterwards a friend suggested that Marilyn should talk to Lee Strasberg who was the director and chief teacher at the Actors Studio in New York. An important new connection, which would last until her death, was made.

It is said that Monroe made Strasberg famous, but he was already a power in the acting world when she joined him. He was the exponent of what came to be known as the "Method" school of acting, derived from the teachings of Konstantin Stanislavsky from the Moscow Art Theater. Many of America's most celebrated actors and film stars had studied with him, the most famous being Marlon Brando. Briefly, the Method suggested that understanding a role was not enough, nor was the ability to make an external projection of what the character might be like. What was needed was an ability to see what was happening inside the character and to be able to re-create that inwardly. This was precisely what Marilyn had been striving for in her sessions with Natasha Lytess and Michael Chekhov. She herself said earlier, "I want to get in touch with my real feelings ... not only in life but in the movies too."

She began by having private lessons with Strasberg. He urged her, as he urged all his students, to go into analysis in the search for their true feelings and she began sessions with psychiatrist Marianne Kris who was also to become a significant person in Marilyn's later years. Later she was able to attend the Actors Studio itself as an observer and on one occasion she performed a scene from Anna Christie with Maureen Stapleton. Marilyn was working hard.

Meanwhile she had renewed her contact with Arthur Miller and they were seeing each other regularly. She met his parents and formed a strong attachment to his father Isadore. She began to make enquiries about converting to Judaism. Ominously, Miller approved neither of Strasberg or of analysis, which, he believed, helped no one and could actually cause damage. Even so, the couple seemed to be progressing inevitably towards marriage.

Meanwhile Greene had, on Marilyn's behalf, pulled off what was recognized in Hollywood as the biggest coup of all time! He had renegotiated her contract with Fox – this time with Marilyn

Bus Stop (1956) is generally considered to be one of Monroe's very best movies. She plays a second-rate saloon singer, with Don Murray as the naive cowboy who sees her as his ideal woman.

Her acting in Bus Stop *(these pages) caused the critics, the public and the Hollywood in-crowd to re-think their views of "that blonde," realising that she actually could act.*

Monroe Productions rather than with her. They had her services for the next seven years for four pictures only at a minimum fee of $100,000 per film. She could also work for herself – for other studios, in television or theatre. She had director (but not script) approval. Her career was now completely under her control.

The first film she would make with Fox under the new agreement would be *Bus Stop*, and her first independent production would be a screenplay based on Terence Rattigan's light comedy *The Sleeping Prince*, re-titled for Marilyn's benefit as *The Prince and the Showgirl*. It was announced that the great British actor (who had starred in the play on stage), Sir Laurence Olivier would not only repeat his role, but also direct the film. Marilyn was distinctly upset about this, feeling, quite rightly, that her newly developing acting technique would be in total conflict with Olivier's more traditional approach. But the offer had been made and publicized, so she unwillingly went along with it. After their first meeting Olivier would write: "She was so adorable, so witty, such incredible fun and more physically attractive than anyone I could have imagined ...." These views would change rapidly when they started working together.

When she returned to Hollywood to begin work on *Bus Stop* it was clear that Marilyn had changed. She herself denied it ("The suit I'm wearing is new, but the girl's the same"), but there was a new air of self-confidence about her, a new serenity. The combined attentions of Strasberg, Kris and Arthur Miller plus her newly acquired business acumen were certainly working. There was one difficulty. Marilyn had hired Lee Strasberg's wife Paula as her coach which meant that Natasha Lytess would be dismissed. This was done tactlessly (a brief telegram from Marilyn Monroe Productions, and no meeting between the two women), Lytess was shattered, left her job at Fox and went back to Europe. She died in Italy in 1964.

Monroe's good/bad performance of "That Old Black Magic" is one of the highlights of Bus Stop *(these pages). She selected her costume herself – insisting on the torn tights. While Monroe was filming* Bus Stop, *her next husband, Arthur Miller, was staying nearby, working on a short story which would eventually be filmed by Monroe.*

Fans were important to Monroe and she always appreciated direct contact with the public. Here she happily signs autographs for children at Idlewild Airport just after her thirtieth birthday.

Most Marilyn students will assert that *Bus Stop* contains her finest performance, even of Oscar-winning caliber. William Inge's 1955 Broadway play was set in an all-night cafe where the passengers on a long-distance bus journey are snow-bound. They each have their own aspirations and needs, but the focus falls on Bo, a naive young rancher who is going to the Big City to find himself the perfect wife, and Cherie, a second-rate nightclub singer whom he sees as his "angel." It is a delicate, moody piece, lightly symbolic in the "bus journey through life" manner.

At least part of the impact Marilyn made in this film was visual. Cherie could easily have become just another one of her not-too-bright-blonde parts. But her search for the inner truth

of the character created an external change. The pink and blonde, sugar-candy doll was banished. Make-up gave her an unhealthy pallor (Cherie works at night, sleeps during the day), her clothes were deliberately tatty, her hair an uncontrolled mess. And it was obvious now that her acting was coming from the inside and not just applied superficially.

Shooting was not terribly happy. Paula Strasberg had taken over from Lytess, but the effect was the same with Marilyn relying entirely on her rather than on director Joshua Logan (who was Marilyn's choice). There was tension, too, between Monroe and her co-star Don Murray a not very well-known young actor who Logan was hoping to make into a star. When filming the snowy location shots, Monroe

A typical Monroe pose at a press conference in New York, taken at the time she and Arthur Miller were making their arrangements to marry.

The summer of 1956 (these pages) was probably the happiest time of Monroe's life. The Miller family offered her a sense of stability and background that had always evaded her, and New York offered a refreshing change from Hollywood. Marilyn got along extremely well with her new parents-in-law: Mrs. Augusta Miller taught her to cook and Isidore remained a close friend right up to Marilyn's death.

insisted on playing her scenes in a thin dress and, inevitably, went down with a virus and acute bronchitis which kept her in hospital for more than two weeks.

Meanwhile Arthur Miller was sitting out the six-week wait for his divorce in Reno. He had taken a cabin at Pyramid Lake and was using the time to write a short story about the people who came to Reno for divorces, to be called *The Misfits* . He and Marilyn were in constant touch at this time. At forty-one, Arthur Miller was considered one of America's finest playwrights (Tennessee Williams being the other). His fame rested, at that time, on *All My Sons* and *Death of a Salesman* , for which he won the Pulitzer Prize and most other major awards. Tall, lean and naturally solemn he seemed to combine all the

characteristics Marilyn looked for in men – with the additional asset of having a close family and a high cultural profile. He and Marilyn were married in a civil ceremony on 29 June, which was followed by a Jewish double-ring ceremony on 1 July. The press went mad and photographs of Marilyn taken at this time against the country background of Miller's farmhouse reveal her undisputed happiness.

But for the third (or fourth?) time, as in some inevitably recurring pattern, this happiness would disappear very soon. Marilyn was now thirty years old – a fact she accepted cheerfully enough – and it was obvious that her days of high glamor would soon be over. If the making of *Bus Stop* was not always happy, this would be nothing compared to the agonies she was to go

Celebration! Marilyn Monroe, her partner Milton Greene (left) and Jack Warner, President of Warner Brothers, announce a distribution deal between his company and Monroe's for her next picture, The Prince and the Showgirl.

through when shooting each of her next four films. To the outside world she seemed simply to be a tiresome, unreliable woman who treated her fellow actors and directors with casual contempt and was probably overdoing the drink and probably the drugs.

Those close to her knew that this was not entirely true (she herself had spent years being treated with contempt by her colleagues). She set impossibly high standards for herself, and so was often almost paralyzed with terror when she ventured before a camera. Also her health was always fragile; she was vulnerable to chest and throat complaints, suffered throughout her life from insomnia and in the late 1940s she was diagnosed as having endometriosis, an abnormal and painful build-up of tissue in the uterus.

Today this complaint can be quite successfully treated, but at that time it was recognized as progressive and would get worse. Most of her pain-killing drugs were prescribed for period pains.

But the troubles over *The Prince and the Showgirl* were due to other things, mainly the build-up of a clash of personalities, eventually centering on Olivier and Monroe, which more or less required the rest of the company and entourage to take sides.

For the newlywed Millers, the trip to London to make the film was, in effect, a honeymoon trip. With them went Lee and Paula Strasberg and Monroe's partner Milton Greene with his wife Amy. Marilyn and Amy were not as close as they had been when Marilyn was living with

Pulling off The Prince and the Showgirl *was a triumph for Marilyn. The movie was to be shot in England, directed by and co-starring Sir Laurence Olivier, so Warner, too, had every right to look pleased.*

Unlike Joe DiMaggio, Arthur Miller (these pages) was seriously interested in his wife's career as a film actress. Although not a man who particularly enjoyed bright lights and socializing, he always supported Monroe when necessary.

Facing page: a routine Warner Brothers publicity shot, released to coincide with the announcement of The Prince and the Showgirl *deal. In London, the Great English Actor and the Great American Sex Goddess (above) presented themselves to the press. Reactions to this unexpected partnership ranged from the derisory to the enthusiastic. Arthur Miller (left) accompanied his wife.*

them. Marilyn was becoming suspicious of Milton and his activities. Miller had no time for the Strasbergs. But, above all, Marilyn was terrified of working with Olivier – not simply because of his status as "the world's greatest actor," but because she knew instinctively that they took diametrically opposed attitudes to acting.

To add to the tension, Marilyn did not go down well with the British press. She was considered reserved and evasive, unwilling to co-operate. Reading reports of the hullabaloo of the arrival at London Airport and the big press conference to launch the film, one is not surprised. She was treated as she used to be treated years before in Hollywood – as a mindless sex-doll, bombarded with inane,

While The Prince and the Showgirl *was shot in England, Arthur and the new Mrs. Miller stayed on a country estate at Englefield Green, Surrey. This was not the happiest time as tensions were growing between them, exacerbated by Monroe's problems with the film.*

insulting questions. There were, too, some barely concealed sneers at her "impudence" in daring to team herself up with the great Olivier and a cast of distinguished British stage actors.

Marilyn's worst fears were confirmed at the start when Olivier wanted two weeks rehearsal so that the cast could get familiar with each other and their material. Like all movie stars, Marilyn was used to working in fragments and the idea scared her out of her wits. As a director Olivier seemed to her patronizing and a bit of a bully. He resented the presence of Paula Strasberg (who was shipped back to America mid-way through production, to be replaced by analyst Marianne Kris).

Inevitably Marilyn began to be increasingly late on the set, often not turning up at all and causing costly delays. But some of the team recognized Marilyn's value. The great actress Dame Sybil Thorndike knew Marilyn was worth waiting for: "She's the only one of us who knows how to act for the camera," she remarked with true professional acumen.

Miller wanted to support his wife, but he also wanted to remain on good terms with Olivier and the British contingent. The United Kingdom was a prime market for his plays where they were given first-class productions and were always well-received (and this remains true to this day). It was at this time that Miller is thought to have begun making notes which would lead to his play *After the Fall*, which would be none too kind to Marilyn. She is said to have discovered the notebook and been shattered by his observations. By the end of the filming, Marilyn's relationship with Milton Greene was on the rocks and fissures were extending through her marriage too.

Rattigan's play juxtaposed an American chorus girl with a stuffy Ruritanian Prince in their search for romance. The film was admired as an elegant piece of work, handsome to look at, and containing a nice performance from Olivier and a deliciously witty one from Monroe, but never really took off at the box office. However, over the years its reputation has increased and it received a new boost when it was shown on British television at the time of Olivier's death. Monroe, it was agreed, simply wiped Olivier off

the screen. This is not entirely true, of course, but in the thirty years which have passed audiences have become totally accepting of the style of Marilyn's acting which, in 1957, was new and different. Olivier seems wooden and word-bound; she seems a free, spontaneous spirit.

England had its compensations for the Millers – Marilyn met the Queen at a Royal Command Performance, there was cycling in Windsor Great Park and a lunch with the eccentric and charismatic poet Edith Sitwell who had met Marilyn in Hollywood and – like Garbo – detected in her an Ophelia-like quality.

It would be well over a year before Marilyn would embark on another film. During this period the Millers made a definite attempt to pull their marriage together. Arthur had bought an authentic colonial farmhouse in Connecticut, and while it was being refurbished they rented a cottage in Amagansett, Long Island. Here, Miller started writing again and Marilyn, as she always did, gave herself to the tranquil pleasures of country living. Soon she discovered she was pregnant, but the joy was short-lived. It turned out to be a tube pregnancy and she lost the baby to save her own life.

As some kind of consolation Miller dedicated himself to the screenplay based on *The Misfits*, which he was writing specifically for her. By July 1958 he had finished the final draft and secured the interest of John Huston as director and had started to pursue Clark Gable for the main role of Gay Langland. Gable, then fifty-nine, was virtually retired but the idea of doing such a remarkable film as his farewell performance attracted him. Miller also found a producer to pull all the threads together.

Marilyn became pregnant again but, inexplicably, contacted Billy Wilder to say she was prepared to work on a film he had put to her earlier. This was *Some Like It Hot*. She did have reservations. For one thing it was to be made in black and white – whereas Marilyn always stipulated color. For another she was completely unsure how to relate to co-stars Jack Lemmon and Tony Curtis who were in drag through most of the film.

Wilder showed her test color shots of Curtis and Lemmon which revealed how utterly

grotesque and vulgar they would look, and of course, she had the experience and taste to agree. Strasberg talked her through the role and gave her valuable hints on how to relate to these strange "girls" which she was happy with.

Some Like It Hot is unquestionably the best film Monroe ever participated in. Whichever way you look at it, it works. Two men who have witnessed a gangland killing (it is set in the 1920s) disguise themselves as women ("Josephine" and "Daphne") and join an all-girls band of which Sugar Kane (Monroe) is the singer. As in all the best farces, one is drawn into the plot in credible stages until it is too late to accuse it of absurdity. It is one of the few Monroe films that does not date. The gender-bending element is handled with exquisite tact

and excellent acting by Curtis and Lemmon. There is no sleeze, no leery nudges, no unsettling undertow of homosexuality or lesbianism. The black and white photography glitters and glimmers. Marilyn never looked more sexy. But the filming was, as ever, fraught. Later, Tony Curtis was to say that kissing Marilyn was like "kissing Hitler," so tyrranically did she insist on perfection.

Again, insecurity and terror struck her making her late on set, sometimes not turning up at all. Moreover she was convinced she looked too fat (she was, after all, pregnant). Director Wilder, who started filming with a great deal of support and tolerance for Marilyn, ended the movie full of rancor – though he and Marilyn eventually made up any differences. A month after shooting

These pages: Sir
Laurence Olivier as
the up-tight prince
regent with Monroe
as Elsie, the American
chorus-girl who uses
her wiles to break
through his facade,
in scenes from The
Prince and the
Showgirl. *The film
was not a big hit
when it was released
in 1957, but over the
years it has been re-
evaluated and is now
regarded as totally
delightful.*

Facing page: Marilyn, wide-eyed with American wonder at stuffy court ceremonies, sits alongside Jeremy Spenser in a scene from The Prince and the Showgirl. *Their return to New York (this page) came as something of a relief to the Millers after the trials and tribulations of filming in England.*

Marilyn wanted to star in the Warner Brothers film of Tennessee Williams' play Baby Doll, *but Carroll Baker got the part. Monroe had no time for resentment and happily agreed to be a Celebrity Usherette (these pages) at a gala performance organized by the famous hostess Perle Mesta. The performance was to benefit the Actors' Studio where Monroe herself had studied.*

Marilyn with Arthur Miller at the "April in Paris" Ball at the Waldorf Astoria in late 1957.

Marilyn Monroe released no films in 1958 – but married life in New York was certainly suiting her, as this radiant snap suggests.

While in New York, Monroe did a remarkable photography session with top photographer Richard Avedon in which she created a series of visual impressions of great stars of the stage and screen. Facing page: her impersonation of Lillian Russell. Above: a press photo from 1958.

was finished it was announced that Marilyn had lost her second baby.

Since her stroll into center-stage with *Niagara* in 1953, every film Marilyn Monroe made had contained something of particular interest – with the exception of *There's No Business Like Showbusiness* . Now she was being pressed to make another musical. She was, of course, contractually bound to Fox for four pictures and the script of *Let's Make Love* was the only one that appealed.

This is probably the worst film that Monroe the star ever made, but not through lack of supporting talent. It was directed by George Cukor and the script was by Norman Krasna. The story was about an off-Broadway company which is joined by a French singer-dancer,

Marilyn Monroe agreed only reluctantly to made Some Like it Hot, *partly because she didn't like the idea of appearing in a black and white movie and partly because she thought her role as Sugar Kane was just another "dim blonde." Facing page: Marilyn takes whispered instruction* from director Billy Wilder. Location shots for Some Like it Hot *were filmed at Coronado Beach (above and overleaf) and the presence of Marilyn ensured a big turnout of fans anxious to catch a glimpse of her. Arthur Miller was in attendance too.*

actually a millionaire, who has fallen for one of the company's actresses and wants to win her heart through honest, rather than financial, means.

For Monroe, the film was just something to get through before she embarked on the far more interesting and demanding project, *The Misfits*. Miller was brought in to tinker with the script and make it more suitable for her talents. Her supporting cast was nothing to write home about with the French singer Yves Montand playing the millionaire and an unknown British singer called Frankie Vaughan in support. Nothing jelled, and the only memorable moment is an extended performance, by Monroe, of Cole Porter's "My Heart Belongs to Daddy" choreographed by her favorite, Jack Cole.

Far more interesting was the back-stage drama. A number of top Hollywood leading men had been approached to play the millionaire, including Gregory Peck, Charlton Heston, Cary Grant and Rock Hudson but all had turned it down. Then along came Yves Montand who had been doing a highly successful one-man song-and-dance show on Broadway. His wife, Simone Signoret was a major star of French movies and about to win the Oscar for her performance in the British film *Room at the Top*. Montand and Signoret had been appearing in Miller's play *The Crucible* for two years and had made the film of the play, called *The Witches of Salem*.

Montand and Monroe immediately proceeded to have an intense affair, but transactions were thoroughly crossed. Montand saw the event as

Marilyn had just refused to pose for a news photographer when this casual shot was taken. She is chatting to Some Like It Hot *co-star, the great comedian Joe E. Brown.*

Words with Billy Wilder at Coronado Beach. Half-hidden by Marilyn is her ever-present coach, Paula Strasberg.

A highlight of Some Like It Hot *is the famous seduction scene between Monroe and Tony Curtis (these pages). Later, notoriously, Curtis was to remark that kissing Marilyn was like kissing Hitler.*

SL(327-3)55

Marilyn on Coronado Beach. During the making of Some Like It Hot *Marilyn was at her most difficult – forgetting her lines and being late for filming. But the film has emerged as one of the great classics of American comedy.*

During her marriage to Arthur Miller, Marilyn had at least two miscarriages – immediately before and soon after the filming of Some Like It Hot. *In June 1959, she spent time in Lenox Hill Hospital for what was described as "gynaecological surgery." The press and her husband were on hand when she was discharged.*

These pages: jumping for joy – an exuberant Monroe performs for the camera of Philippe Halsman in New York, 1959.

Monroe agreed to
appear in Let's Make
Love to fulfil her
contract with
Twentieth Century
Fox. Also in the cast
was the young British
pop singer Frankie
Vaughan.

Another English member of the Let's Make Love *cast was the delightful Wilfrid Hyde-White (right).*

Marilyn's co-star and romantic lead was the French actor and singer Yves Montand.

Let's Make Love
*(these pages) is
considered, today, to
be perhaps the least
impressive film to
which Monroe lent
her talents. The only
memorable moments
are the song-and-
dance routines,
including an
elaborate re-working
of Cole Porter's classic
"My Heart Belongs to
Daddy."*

These pages and overleaf left: Marilyn Monroe and Yves Montand in scenes from Let's Make Love. During the making of this film, the couple's off-stage romantic involvement was more interesting than the fictional one on the screen.

Monroe and Montand at a New York party. Later Montand was to say "Perhaps she had a schoolgirl crush. If she did, I'm sorry. But nothing will break up my marriage." And, sure enough, having enjoyed his affair with Monroe, he returned to his wife, the actress Simone Signoret.

an amusing diversion: his wife, Simone Signoret clearly never imagined he would leave her (and he didn't). Monroe, even though still married to Arthur Miller invested Montand with all the magic she decided would be needed by the next man in her life.

Eventually Montand extricated himself from the affair with Gallic finesse, though this was not too kind to Marilyn whom he said had a "school-girl" crush on him, and returned to Signoret. For Marilyn it was a hard lesson in itself, but a clear signal that her marriage to Arthur Miller was over.

A divorce was not filed, however, until *The Misfits* was over. It could not possibly have been known at the time, but this was the last film Monroe would complete. On paper it sounds

Facing page: Marilyn eyes her Golden Globe Award, given by the Hollywood Foreign Press Association for her performance as "Best Actress in a Motion Picture Comedy" in the film Some Like It Hot. *The Foreign Press Association had named her "The World Film Favorite" in 1953 and repeated the honor in 1961.* The Misfits *(above) (1961) was the last film Marilyn was to complete. She had a nervous breakdown while filming and, despite her impending divorce from him, Arthur Miller – who wrote the script – was there on set. The director (left) was John Huston.*

Monroe and Clark
Gable in The Misfits.
She had always
adored him ever since
she was a child,
fantasizing then that
he was her father.

brilliant, an unmissable line-up with John Huston directing and cast that includes Clark Gable, Montgomery Clift, Eli Wallach and Thelma Ritter. Add to that the fact that the script was originally intended to be a loving present from Miller to Monroe.

The film received indifferent and mixed notices. But over the years its reputation has grown – but more because it represents an image of the past rather than a pointer to the future. Throughout the filming, Monroe was in a fragile state. She had a nervous and physical breakdown which led to the closing of the production for a week. She returned and after a week, collapsed again. Meanwhile Miller met the woman who would be his next (and final) wife, the photographer Inge Morath there to cover the filming.

One consolation to Marilyn during the fraught filming was the friendship which developed between her and Clark Gable. She had had him marked down as a surrogate father from her pre-teen years and now she was working with him as a co-star.

He was continually gentle, kind, understanding and supportive. When he died of a heart attack after filming was finished it was suggested that Marilyn was responsible for the tension which provoked the crisis. She was, of course, desperately upset by this accusation. Gable was an old, experienced Hollywood performer, on *The Misfits* he was cool and laid back, enjoying this chance, late in his career, to play the cowboy.

The last year of Marilyn Monroe's life was turbulent and troubled. Professionally it was not a good time for her. The poor reception given to *Let's Make Love* followed by the curiously underestimated *The Misfits* prompted the idea that she was past her peak and that her screen career was on the decline. Her nervous breakdown during the making of the latter film, followed by her divorce from Arthur Miller and then the death of Clark Gable shattered her already tenuous grasp on reality.

She returned to New York to try and pick up the threads of her life. There were plenty of offers but the only project she was interested in was a television production of the play *Rain* , to be directed by Lee Strasberg. This came to nothing because NBC would not employ Strasberg since he had no television experience and Monroe would not work without him.

There as one particularly distressing episode. After reading that Kay Gable was suggesting that Monroe's behavior had led to her husband's heart attack, Marilyn came very close to suicide. As a result her analyst Marianne Kris suggested she enter the Payne Whitney Psychiatric Clinic in New York.

Although she knew what kind of clinic this was, and although she went voluntarily she had not realized that she would be held in the same conditions as the severely mentally-ill cases. The bleak surroundings, constant supervision and total lack of privacy threw her into a panic. She was allowed one telephone call and she used to contact Joe DiMaggio who immediately flew to New York and managed to extricate her and see her removed to the more comfortable Columbia Presbyterian Hospital. Released from there she spent time with Joe DiMaggio at Fort Lauderdale, resting and fishing.

Her days in New York were clearly over for the time being. In April she closed down her apartment and returned to Hollywood, unsettled and depressed. Her friends tried to cheer her up. Frank Sinatra was around and gave her a white poodle which she named "Maf" – short for Mafia (a joke Sinatra may or may not have appreciated). She was adopted by the "rat pack" – the group of high-livers led by Sinatra, Peter Lawford and Sammy Davis Jr.

But she was finding it difficult to pull herself back to her usual vitality and became increasingly reliant on her doctor, Hyman Engelberg, and her analyst, Ralph Greenson. In May part of her pancreas was removed, and in June her gall bladder was removed.

Other people were entering her life too, notably the Kennedy brothers. Their sister Pat was married to Peter Lawford and Monroe was beginning to treat her as her best friend. She met a lot of the Kennedy clan at the Lawfords' beach house. Dr. Greenson felt that Marilyn needed a housekeeper and urged her to hire a friend of his, Eunice Murray. It has been suggested that this was a move by Greenson to get someone in Marilyn's home who would let him know her state of mind or any significant changes in her moods. The two women took to each other at once – Marilyn brought out Mrs. Murray's maternal instincts and she stayed with her when Marilyn moved into a house she bought the following year.

The Misfits has been described as "a work of collective genius" but the film never really worked. Clark Gable, the male star, died less than two weeks after the film's completion and, as we now know through hindsight, Montgomery Clift and Marilyn Monroe were also doomed. Facing page: Monroe has split from Miller and attends the film's premier with co-star Clift.

During the last years of her life, Marilyn Monroe was in and out of various hospitals, usually for what was described as "physical and emotional exhaustion." Here she leaves the Columbia Presbyterian Hospital after a three-week stay in 1961.

Marilyn reports for duty on the set of what would have been her thirtieth film, Something's Got To Give *(1962). After the emotional and physical problems of the last year she has lost some 15lbs in weight and the magic remains.*

These pages and overleaf left: scenes from Something's Got To Give. *Marilyn was fired and then re-hired during stormy attempts to get the film off the ground. Finally, some ten minutes of her work were filmed and can be seen in the tribute film* Marilyn *released soon after her death and narrated by Rock Hudson.*

She still owed Fox two pictures under her contract and they sent her the script of a movie called *Something's Got to Give* which was a remake of a 1940 comedy (starring Cary Grant and Irene Dunne) about a shipwrecked wife, presumed dead who reappears to find her husband has just remarried. Nunnally Johnson had re-fashioned the script. Monroe agreed to do it.

Moving into the house Mrs. Murray had found for her occupied some of her time. It was, incidentally, the first home Marilyn actually owned herself – a small, secluded Mexican-style villa tucked away on Fifth Helena Avenue. "My fortress" Marilyn would call it.

As the first day of shooting on Something's Got to Give approached Marilyn went down with

influenza. She had been eating little, had lost fifteen pounds and as close-ups taken at this period show, looked almost gaunt. The studio had made considerable efforts to make things comfortable for the star. The producer was Henry Weinstein who was a friend of Dr. Greenson. George Cukor, who had handled Marilyn nicely on *Let's Make Love* was to direct. One of her "rat pack" friends, Dean Martin was the leading man. But there were problems with the script. Marilyn had liked the first Nunnally Johnson draft she had seen but since then many revisions had altered it. Marilyn never had script approval built into her contract but it was known that if she did not like a script she simply would not turn up.

To everyone's surprise she did turn up for the

The press was called in to photograph a swimming pool sequence in Something's Got To Give. *During the session, Marilyn slipped out of her flesh-colored swimming costume and presented herself naked to the cameras.*

In June 1962, the photographer Bert Stern was commissioned to do a photo session with Marilyn for Vogue magazine, which included nude, semi-nude and fashion shots. This is sometimes referred to as "The Last Sitting."

However, at the same time, Marilyn Monroe also posed at Santa Monica for photographer George Barris. These pictures reveal that the Monroe allure and magic were still very much in evidence (overleaf left). Incredibly, a few weeks later she would be dead.

The secluded house where Marilyn died. It was the first home she had ever owned. Right: the bedroom, where she was found naked, clutching a telephone, in the early hours of August 5, 1962, was far from completely furnished.

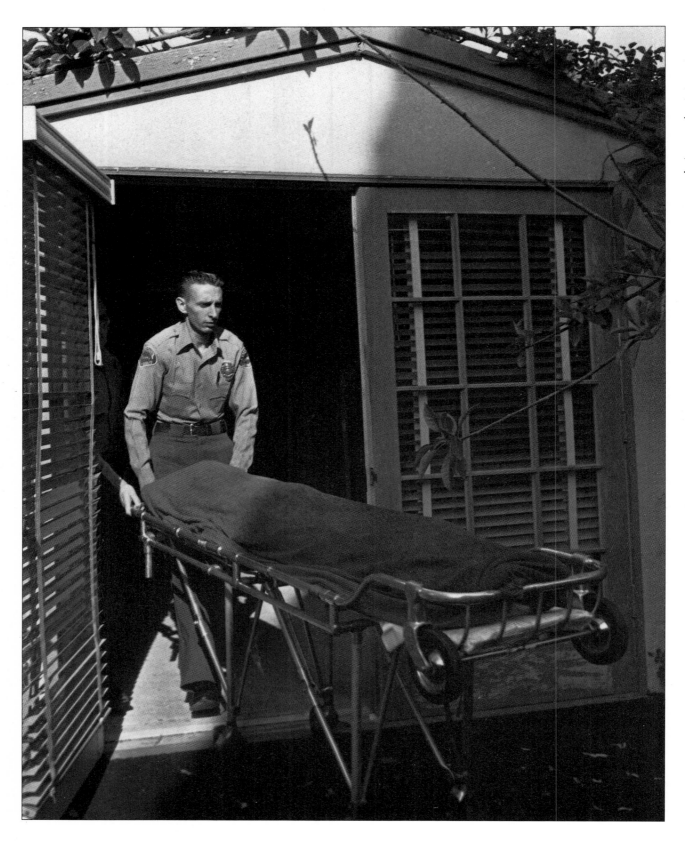

These pages: the aftermath of death. Facing page bottom: a policeman checks Marilyn's belongings – such as her jewellery and furs – into safekeeping, while the body (this page) is transferred from the mortuary to the morgue.

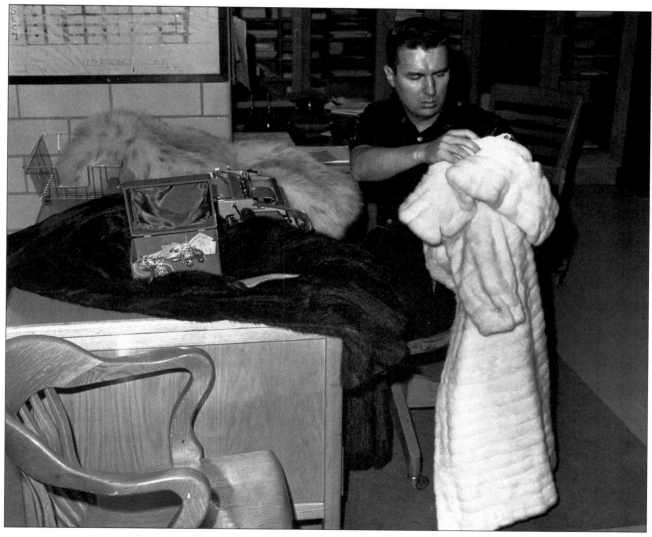

Monroe's funeral (these pages) was organized by Joe DiMaggio, who kept the event a very private affair. No show-business friends of Marilyn were there and the crowd of fans waiting to see the coffin arrive was small. Facing page: DiMaggio's grief was very evident. He ordered that fresh red roses should be placed, twice a week, in a vase on the crypt where his ex-wife was finally laid to rest.

first day of shooting, but not the second. After five weeks, during which only seven minutes of usable footage of Marilyn was captured, she was fired. One incident during the filming which did not endear her to the studio was that, after days absent from the set she flew to New York to appear at a birthday gala for President Kennedy. Sewn into one of "skin and bead" dresses, she very slowly and very breathily whispered through the song "Happy Birthday" before the throng in Madison Square Garden. She was escorted by her close friend Isadore Miller – Arthur's father.

For a brief evening the old Marilyn image was restored – glittering, incandescent. Another flash of the old, vital Marilyn happened on the set. There was a photo-call for a shot where Marilyn is swimming in a pool, supposedly naked. But nudity was not allowed on the screen so she had to wear a flesh colored swimming costume. Once in the water, however, Marilyn wriggled out of her costume and to the amazed delight of the cameramen swam around naked. Within a few years nudity would be commonplace on the screen, but at this point Marilyn was pioneering. The pictures appeared in magazines in thirty-two countries.

Marilyn's thirty-sixth birthday was celebrated by the cast and crew on 1 June and that happened to be also the very last day's work she ever did. Marilyn kept herself busy. In July she did a nude session for photographer Bert Stern which are among the loveliest ever taken of her, and she gave a long interview to *Life* magazine.

Previous pages, these pages, overleaf right and following pages: the enduring images – the pin-up girl who became an actress whose films will remain fresh forever.

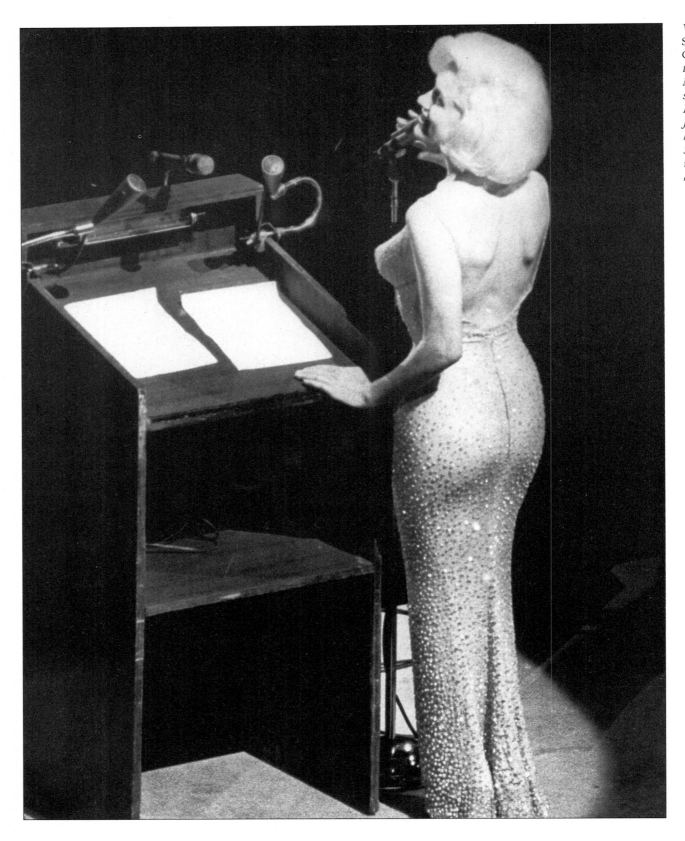

While filming Something's Got To Give, *Marilyn took time off to fly over to New York, where she sang "Happy Birthday" to President John F. Kennedy at his party at Madison Square Garden. She was sewn into her dress.*

She was seeing Joe DiMaggio, Frank Sinatra, the Kennedy brothers and other men. Late in the month she entered the Cedars of Lebanon Hospital, allegedly for an abortion.

In the early hours of the morning on 5 August Marilyn was found dead in her bedroom. She had been playing Frank Sinatra records, she was naked and the telephone was clutched in her hand. On 18 August the Suicide Investigation Team announced that she had died from a drug overdose.

There are three possible explanations of Monroe's death. She deliberately committed suicide. She took an accidental overdose of drugs. She was murdered and the scene arranged to make it appear as if she had committed suicide.

Each of these theories has been exhaustively explored in the millions of words that have been written about her over the last thirty years. The murder/conspiracy theory involves the Kennedy brothers and her connections with the Mafia. But whatever the truth, there was certainly something not quite right about the scene of her death and much unresolved speculation about who visited her that night and who she was calling on the telephone. The coroner was accused of failing to perform the autopsy thoroughly. Over the years prime witnesses have died, others have changed their stories. Possibly the truth will never be known.

The faithful Joe DiMaggio stepped in to take charge of the funeral arrangements. It was a small, private ceremony at the Westwood

Memorial Park Chapel. The guests included a
few of her long-standing friends (Anne Karger,
Paula Strasberg) but there were no Hollywood
stars – Sinatra, Ella Fitzgerald, the Lawfords were
among those excluded. Marilyn's make-up man
Whitey Snyder made up her face and she was
dressed in her favorite green Pucci dress. The
music was Judy Garland singing "Over the
Rainbow."

(Note: The dates refer to the year of release, not the year in which the film may have been made.)

1. *Scudda Hoo! Scudda Hay!* (1948)
Director: F. Hugh Herbert
Stars: June Haver, Lon McCallister
Marilyn's brief scenes were cut. She can be seen in a rowing boat during one sequence.

2. *Dangerous Years* (1947)
Director: Arthur Pierson
Stars: William Halop, Ann E. Todd
Marilyn has a brief scene as a waitress.

3. *Ladies of the Chorus* (1948)
Director: Phil Karlson
Stars: Adele Jergens, Rand Brooks
Her first substantial part and her first singing role.

4. *Love Happy* (1950)
Director: David Miller
Stars: The Marx Brothers, Vera-Ellen
Her short scene with Groucho introduced the famous wiggle to the world.

5. *A Ticket to Tomahawk* (1950)
Director: Richard Sale
Stars: Dan Dailey, Anne Baxter
Marilyn played a chorus girl.

6. *The Asphalt Jungle* (1950)
Director: John Huston
Stars: Sterling Hayden, Louis Calhern
A cameo performance which caught wide attention.

7. *All about Eve* (1950)
Director: Joseph L. Mankiewicz
Stars: Bette Davis, Anne Baxter, George Sanders
Another cameo role which opened the door to future stardom.

8. *The Fireball* (1950)
Director: Tay Garnett
Stars: Mickey Rooney, Pat O'Brien
A roller-skating epic.

9. *Right Cross* (1950)
Director: John Sturges
Stars: June Allyson, Dick Powell
Marilyn was wasted in a trivial bit part.

10. *Hometown Story* (1951)
Director: Arthur Pierson
Stars: Jeffrey Lynn, Donald Crisp
Propaganda movie promoting American industry.

11. *As Young As You Feel* (1951)
Director: Harmon Jones
Stars: Monty Woolley, Constance Bennett
Marilyn was a secretary in this unpretentious comedy.

12. *Love Nest* (1951)
Director: Joseph Newman
Stars: William Lundigan, June Haver
The blonde home-wrecker.

13. *Let's Make It Legal* (1951)
Director: Richard Sale
Stars: Claudette Colbert, Zachary Scott
Marilyn as the blonde gold-digger.

14. *Clash by Night* (1952)
Director: Fritz Lang
Stars: Barbara Stanwyck, Robert Ryan
Marilyn introduces blue jeans in working-class drama.

15. *We're Not Married* (1952)
Director: Edmund Goulding
Stars: Ginger Rogers, Mitzi Gaynor, Zsa Zsa Gabor
Marilyn as a beauty contest winner.

16. *Don't Bother to Knock* (1952)
Director: Roy Baker
Co-star: Richard Widmark
As a psychotic baby-sitter, a role departure for Monroe.

17. *Monkey Business* (1952)
Director: Howard Hawks
Stars: Cary Grant, Ginger Rogers
Back to the blonde secretary.

18. O Henry's *Full House*
Director: Henry Koster
Co-star: Charles Laughton
The streetwalker and the tramp.

19. *Niagara* (1953)
Director: Henry Hathaway
Co-star: Joseph Cotton
The build-up really starts here, with Marilyn as a murderous wife.

20. *Gentlemen Prefer Blondes* (1953)
Director: Howard Hawks
Co-star: Jane Russell
Prime vehicle for Marilyn. The musical that confirmed her star status.

21. *How to Marry a Millionaire* (1953)
Director: Jean Negulesco
Co-stars: Betty Grable, Lauren Bacall
Gold-digging comedy with Marilyn as the short-sighted blonde.

22. *River of No Return* (1954)
Director: Otto Preminger
Co-star: Robert Mitchum
Adventure western with a child and songs.

23. *There's No Business Like Showbusiness* (1954)
Director: Walter Lang
Co-stars: Ethel Merman, Dan Dailey, Donald O'Connor
Indifferent back-stage musical.

24. *The Seven Year Itch* (1955)
Director: Billy Wilder
Co-star:Tom Ewell
Marilyn's comic talents are beginning to be recognized.

25. *Bus Stop* (1956)
Director: Joshua Logan
Co-star: Don Murray
Another dramatic role, requiring tenderness and tackiness.

26. *The Prince and the Showgirl* (1957)
Director: Laurence Olivier
Co-star: Laurence Olivier
Pedestrian comedy that improves with age.

27. *Some Like It Hot* (1959)
Director: Billy Wilder
Co-stars: Tony Curtis, Jack Lemmon
Arguably Monroe's most brilliant comic performance.

28. *Let's Make Love* (1960)
Director: George Cukor
Co-star: Yves Montand
Lack-lustre musical.

29. *The Misfits* (1961)
Director: John Huston
Co-stars: Clark Gable, Montgomery Clift
Arthur Miller wrote it for her.

30. *Something's Got to Give*
Director; George Cukor
Co-stars: Dean Martin, Cyd Charisse
Never completed. The few minutes of existing footage is sometimes seen on television.

There are literally hundreds of books about Marilyn Monroe, some serious, many exploitative and trashy. This is a highly selective list of the better ones.

Marilyn, a biography by Norman Mailer (1973)
Imaginative, speculative, appreciative. Much of Mailer's conjectures have since been elaborated upon and confirmed.

Norma Jeane: The Life and Death of Marilyn Monroe, by Fred Lawrence Guiles (revised edition, 1985).
The classic biography. Thoroughly researched, measured in tone, sympathetic but not besotted.

Goddess: The Secret Lives of Marilyn Monroe, by Anthony Summers (1985)
Epic in scale, the fullest and most detailed factual account of every known aspect of Monroe's life which is likely to be produced. The murder conspiracy theories are explored in depth.

The Marilyn Conspiracy, by Milo Speriglio and Steven Chain (1986)
Almost a thriller. Speriglio spent thirteen years trying to track down the truth about Monroe's death. Convincing, disturbing.

The Marilyn Scandal, by Sandra Shevey (1987)
An interpretation of Marilyn's life from a feminist point of view, revealing her as a pioneer, a new woman years before her time. Not always accurate on small details but a good read.

The Unabridged Marilyn, by Randall Riese and Neal Hitchens (1987)
A dedicated encyclopaedia of every known fact about Monroe from a list of her lovers to her favorite shade of nail polish and what her eating habits were. A must for every fan!